Beyond Mid-Life Crisis

A Psychodynamic Approach to Ageing

BEYOND MID-LIFE CRISIS

A Psychodynamic Approach to Ageing

Peter Hildebrand

sheldon PRESS

First published in Great Britain in 1995 by
Sheldon Press, SPCK, Marylebone Road, London NW1 4DU

British Library Cataloguing-in-Publication Data
A catalogue record for this book is available from the British Library
ISBN 0-85969-702-9

Typeset by Deltatype Ltd, Ellesmere Port, Cheshire
Printed in Great Britain by Biddles Ltd, Guildford and King's Lynn

I wish to dedicate this book to my friend and colleague, the late Naomi Stern, whose friendship I valued greatly, and whose thoughtful contributions helped make this book possible.

| *Contents*

Acknowledgements

This book would not have been written without the help of many friends and colleagues with whom I have worked on the problems of ageing over the last twenty years.

I wish to thank George Pollock, who made it possible for me to enjoy a semi-sabbatical in Chicago in 1977 and to meet and learn from David Guttman, Jerome Grunes and Mort Liebermann, who became both collaborators and valued friends.

In London, Enid Balint and Adam Limentani contributed much to my development as a psychoanalyst, while David Malan and John Wilson taught me a great deal about brief psycho-therapy. Bob Gosling supported me loyally when I first started my workshop for older patients at the Tavistock, and many others contributed to our work. Inge Wise was the perfect partner in marital therapy – calm, thoughtful, and committed to our work together. My secretaries, Beatty Gellert and Jenny Benedict offered me more than I deserved in the way of kindness, sympathy and support.

My wife, Maggie Mills, brings her keen mind and capacity for conceptualization to the work which we have done, and has always been a constructive critic of this work, while my children and stepchildren have provided me with a happy environment within which I could find the time and energy to write this book. My debt to them is greater than I can express here.

The Mount Fund gave us several grants and have always been generous in their support of this work. In particular they supported Naomi Stern's participation in the project.

I am grateful to the Tavistock Clinic for allowing me to use some of my clinical time for the Workshop on the Second Half of Life which I conducted from 1977 to 1990. It is a continuing sadness to me that the challenge presented by research and development of work with people in the Third Age was too much for an institution which I have watched dwindle from a power-house of ideas for applied psychoanalysis towards an enduring and seemingly incurable mediocrity.

Joanna Moriarty has been a patient and helpful editor, and I am grateful to the Sheldon Press for making this book possible.

Introduction

I wish in this book to present a psychodynamically informed approach to ageing. I have many reasons for wanting to give my work in this field a more permanent base than leaving it buried in the pages of the technical journals, good as these are. But apart from a narcissistic and understandable wish to write up this work, I believe that one of the ways in which psychotherapy and psychoanalysis can offer a real contribution to our culture is to undertake both therapeutic and research studies into later life and its problems.

I do not doubt that this will come up against enormous resistances. I have pleasant memories of serving on the board of the *International Journal of Psychoanalysis*, when the topic of categorizing the articles came up. On several occasions I have urged the importance of having a category which I called 'Life-span developmental psychology', which would include work with older patients. This was always received with interest and applause, but whenever any list of categories appears, I search for it without success. Similarly, although the Tavistock Clinic allowed me to use some of my time to set up a workshop for brief psychotherapy with older patients, they never allotted me any professional staff, and the workshop was entirely staffed by external students and visiting fellows. It seems to me that because of the infantomorphic and child-centred nature of psychoanalytic theorizing, the fact that people can and do make major changes in their psychology and psychopathology in later life is an awkward fact that many find hard to digest and accept.

I have tried to show in this book that this is a shortsighted and unfortunate point of view. I suggest that in some senses it derives from an attitude about creativity which is inappropriate to modern psychoanalytic theory. One of my major themes throughout the book is my desire to underline the fact that creativity does not diminish as we age. The crucial lesson that I and my colleagues have learned has been that there is a capacity for change and development in all of us, and that close attention to the ageing process can give access to the same capacity. Whether one takes an economic, dynamic or genetic point of view, psychotherapy and other psychological approaches to the problems of those in later life is well justified and worthwhile. Clearly, as ways of observing and learning change and develop throughout life, insights will in the same way change and develop, and we will need to develop new ways of interpreting and deepening them. It is here that the work of the dynamic psychotherapist will come into its own.

If I had to lay out a therapeutic plan for the future, I would at once ensure that we had a cadre of trained therapists who were capable of developing and deepening our understanding of later life and its problems. What is needed is greater public recognition of the emerging importance of the years between 50 and 75, which the French have christened the Third Age. Human beings in our time are enjoying and living through a period for which there are no precedents, and we have to begin to deepen our understanding of the psychological variables which are involved.

What I have tried to do in this book is to expound a philosophy of therapy which can be enlarged to help us understand the problems involved in growing old in our century. We can look forward to a period of time in the First World when it should be possible for the ageing population in the Third Age to demand and achieve a leisure-based period of creativity and service which will be far longer and more productive than any similar group has achieved. What people do with it will be fascinating to see, provided they are not treated as second-class citizens, but rather both envied and assisted to achieve what is open to them. I am thinking here of retirement communities in the United States where some members of these groups spend much of their time in creative and helpful pursuits which are very different from the average dream of retiring to the south and spending time in the sunshine eating, drinking and playing cards and golf. While those for whom this is an acceptable goal should of course be free to follow such a course, it seems a waste of opportunity to devote these years to narcissistic self-indulgence.

People in the Third Age may have their biggest impact not as workers but as consumers and voters. It is not a homogeneous population, and most will not be rich, but even so they will en masse have more disposable income than any other group. They will spend more of their income on time rather than on possessions: time to travel, to study, to play, and time to keep healthy. They will also bring with them enormous problems about their roles, since there are no real definitions of how or to what end they can or should use their experience. Many of them will need counselling or therapy as they work out the possibilities and limitations of what is available to them.

In the past we have far too uncritically accepted an hypothesis of continuous physical and intellectual development with a rising curve of growth from birth to adulthood, a long refractory period and then a terminal stage of psychic deficit and social withdrawal preliminary to dying and death itself. We have come to understand that this theory is far too simplistic, and that the years of a person's life between the mid-30s and old age are very far from constituting an unchanging and stable period.

This period is regarded by many as one of deficit. Let me quote a journalistic account of masculine ageing:

> ... the hormone production levels are dropping, the head is balding, sexual vigour is diminishing, the stress is unending, the parents are dying, the job horizons are narrowing, the friends are having their first heart attacks: the past floats by in a fog of hopes not realized, opportunities not grasped, women not bedded, potentials not fulfilled and the future is the confrontation with one's own mortality.[1]

In the same way as simplistic accounts of the menopause attribute many physical and psychological phenomena of middle life in women to a discrete physiological cause, so this unhappy picture of ageing concentrates on physiology and minimizes a number of psychological transitional phases which are more or less common to all individuals in later life.

I take an opposite view. For me human ageing is a very complex process, which we are very far from understanding completely. It is clear that human beings display a multitude of developmental characteristics, all of which may change more or less markedly under the influence of both the internal and external psychological environments. Today, in the Western world the post-parental phase of robust physical health has been greatly extended for most people, while the proportion of the population over the age of 40 has increased significantly. Nowadays, for the first time men and women can look forward to 30 or 50 years of productive life after their children have reached adulthood. As a result of this major change in social patterns, two-thirds of married couples over the age of 75 live on their own rather than as part of an extended family.

> We live today in a society: . . . that is becoming accustomed to 70-year-old students, 30-year-old college presidents, 22-year-old mayors, 35-year-old grandmothers, 50-year-old retirees, 65-year-old fathers of pre-schoolers, 60-year olds and 30-year olds wearing the same clothing styles and 85-year-old parents caring for 65-year-old offspring . . .[2]

This has led to further pressure on the individual in the second half of life. His or her secure pattern of life has been disrupted, and economic or political circumstances may threaten or even destroy job security; personal identity is equally threatened by the unstable, and at times seemingly chaotic world in which he finds himself. This situation is unprecedented in our cultural history. Along with this goes a marked alteration in the attitude which society holds towards the elderly. It is a truism to say that ours is a youth culture, but it is worth remembering that in a youth culture those who are not young feel themselves at a psychological disadvantage.

Recent theoretical advances are leading us towards a far more complex definition of the ageing process, so that we no longer think of ageing in purely chronological terms. While chronological age is a useful marker, it has become clear that we must also think about ageing in biological, physiological, cognitive, socio-economic, cultural and psychological terms:

> . . . while the individual in a simple society has a life course which is laid out for him, the individual in our own society, within socially set limits, creates his own life course. Thus both the nature and the timing of major life roles involves a complex interaction between individual choices and the range of social options available.[3]

A series of researches suggests that most older individuals accommodate more or less well to a kind of sexual bi-modality, and begin to live out and even to enjoy the hitherto submerged aspects of the self:

Men are free to live out feminine aspects of the self that they previously had to submerge in the service of their particular parental task, while women regain a masculine potential which was previously submerged or lived out vicariously through identification with the prestige and exploits of the husband. Thus each sex re-establishes a sexual bi-modality that was previously parcelled out externally between the self and the spouse. This leads towards the normal androgeny of later life.

Men may become more openly sensual, dependent and emotional; women can become happily assertive, less needful of love, and more ready to risk the loss of love in trials of strength. In many cases, these post-parental psychological shifts lead eventually to growth, the emergence of new capacities for enjoyment, new sensitivities, and new executive capacities for each sex. While this change towards increased androgeny in later life is psychologically important and satisfying for many, for some it may present every sort of psychological problem. For example, for the man who is struggling with uncertainty about his work future and having to give up long-cherished ideals in terms of money, achievement, and so on, the pressures of the competitive wife released from the demands of child-rearing and homemaking may become enormously difficult.

The problems which may arise in later life as a result of these new challenges are both new and a replay of old conflicts. To some extent they are reactivations of previous patterns of experience, with their roots in early experiences in childhood and infancy. The child's reactions to significant figures and behaviours may well be suppressed or held in abeyance by strong defences for decades, only to emerge under the stress of new phase-appropriate pressures of later life. In men we commonly see problems such as depression, anxiety, sexual acting-out and deviance, alcoholism and psychosomatic illness. Women present many similar problems of depression and hypochondriasis, with its emphasis on the importance of the 'sick role' as responses to the threat of isolation and loss of important figures in the woman's life. C. G. Jung put the matter very clearly:

This is what makes the transition . . . so terribly difficult and bitter for many people: they cling to the illusion of youth or to their children hoping in this way to salvage a last scrap of youth

... it is a sort of second puberty, not infrequently accompanied by tempests of passion, the dangerous age.[4]

Recent evidence suggests that there is an adult developmental process which takes place in us all. In later adulthood, the events I have described briefly above may often disrupt previously adaptive systems with challenges which lead to conflict, tension and potentially the evolution of new and more satisfactory solutions, leading to changes in the way we think about ourselves and our relationships to others. It is easy but too facile to describe them in pathological terms, since many people resolve some if not all of these problems in ways which are creative and satisfying to both themselves and others. In this book I discuss the ways in which people come to terms with such challenges – the need to accept and optimize their own life and achievements, consider them as meaningful, and continue to develop their own skills and capacities within their actual physical capacities.

Working with such people I feel that we can begin to examine and enjoy the dynamics of later life in an authentic sense. They teach us the value of the understated, of quiet growth, of new sorts of creativity. If the Kleinian notion of the depressive position has value, then the continued struggle with presence and absence, with reconciling what one has and what one has lost, is indeed an experience which it is crucial to repeat again and again throughout life. I maintain that such work with older adults is truly therapeutic. Far from holding that the normal problems of later life should be ignored or only treated chemically or behaviourally, I consider that the psychological issues raised by the Third Age have their own validity. The neglect and misunderstanding of the experience of older people can only impoverish our theory, our practice and our ability to live in harmony with one another. The true importance of understanding the psychodynamics of later life is that they enable us to complete and enrich our understanding of human experience as a dynamic unity.

Hopefully, as people age they can accept conflict as inevitable, and recognize the needs and capacities of others as well as their own. The qualities which seem to be required to come to terms with the problems of later life include such notions as grace, patience and wisdom, to enable us to care for others and enable them to develop in their own ways and time. We have to know when to intervene and when to stand back and let others have their say, when to intervene and when to retreat into our own inner worlds. Ageing is an intricate, delicate and on-going process, in which we and others constantly interact with and confront our solutions from the past, our prejudices from the present and the pressures from inside and outside. Many themes will emerge and the developmental picture turns out, in fact to be as complex as that of our early years. In the rest of this book I will select some major areas of developmental conflict and try and describe the solutions which people may achieve.

1
Dynamic Approaches to Ageing

We have come to accept that adulthood is not a monolithic stage which stretches from receiving 'the key to the door' at 18 or 21 to retirement and a gold watch at an age somewhere between 65 and 70. Psychological theorists have subjected adulthood to a great deal of study and description; we would feel nowadays that Shakespeare's seven ages of man would be a somewhat simplistic description of a complex process. In one of his early works, Erik Erikson, perhaps the most influential of all psychoanalytic writers on this topic, put forward the notion that adulthood might be divided into three major stages of early, middle and late. Colarusso and Nemiroff adopted this idea and set out a range of psychological tasks appropriate to each of these stages (Figure 1). Reading from the bottom, you can see the gradual development from the late teens through to the late-adult transition, which commences in the 60s. Let me try and spell out what this implies for both men and women.

Early Adulthood

In the first stage of adult development there are various tasks which we need to complete in order to ease our development into fully functioning adults. The authors of this chart suggest that we have to attempt some or all of the following tasks.

We have to begin to separate psychologically from our parents so that we may begin to develop a feeling of our own integrity and uniqueness as people in our own right, and not just members of a certain hierarchy in our families of origin. In a celebrated *New Yorker* cartoon, an old lady rushes up to the lifeguard saying, 'Quick, quick, my-son-the-doctor is drowning!' The son has some important psychological work to do if he survives the physical threat of drowning, which may be preferable to being swamped by his mother's complete possession of him as an object of her phantasy. The notion that the function of children is to give

DEVELOPMENTAL PERIODS

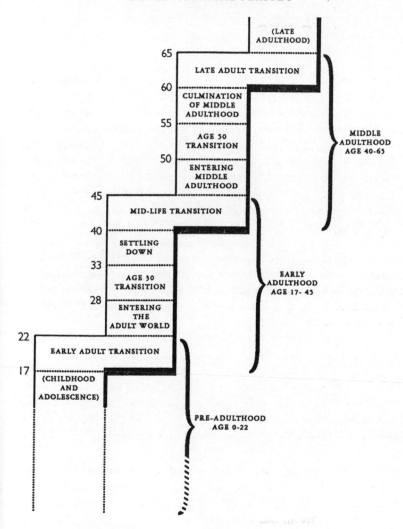

Figure 1. Developmental periods in early and middle adulthood[5]

their parents 'joy' represents an often mutual reluctance to relinquish close family bonding in favour of autonomy for both parents and children.

Figure 2. Individual and marital stages of development[6]

	Stage 1 (18–21 years)	Stage 2 (22–28 years)	Stage 3 (29–31 years)
Individual stage	Pulling up roots	Provisional adulthood	Transition at age 30
Individual task	Developing autonomy	Developing intimacy and occupational identification: 'getting into the adult world'	Deciding about commitment to work and marriage
Marital task	Shift from family of origin to new commitment	Provisional marital commitment	Commitment crisis: restlessness
Marital conflict	Original family ties conflict with adaptation	Uncertainty about choice of marital partner: stress over parenthood	Doubts about choice come into sharp conflict: rates of growth may diverge if spouse has not successfully negotiated stage 2 because of parental obligations
Intimacy	Fragile intimacy	Deepening but ambivalent intimacy	Increasing distance while partners make up their minds about each other
Power	Testing of power	Establishment of patterns of conflict resolution	Sharp vying for power and dominance
Marital boundaries	Conflicts over in-laws	Friends and potential lovers: work versus family	Temporary disruptions including extra-marital sex or reactive 'fortress building'

Stage 4 (32–39 years)	Stage 5 (40–42 years)	Stage 6 (43–59 years)	Stage 7 (60 years and over)
Settling down	Midlife transition	Middle adulthood	Older age
Deepening commitments: pursuing more long-range goals	Searching for 'fit' between aspirations and environment	Re-establishing and re-ordering priorities	Dealing effectively with ageing, illness, and death while retaining zest for life
Productivity: children, work, friends, and marriage	Summing up: success and failure are evaluated and future goals sought	Resolving conflicts and stabilizing the marriage for the long haul	Supporting and enhancing each other's struggle for productivity and fulfilment in face of the threats of ageing
Husband and wife have different and conflicting ways of achieving productivity	Husband and wife perceive 'success' differently: conflict between individual success and remaining in the marriage	Conflicting rates and directions of emotional growth: concerns about losing youthful-ness may lead to depression and/or acting out	Conflicts are generated by rekindled fears of desertion, loneliness, and sexual failure
Marked increase in intimacy in 'good' marriages: gradual distancing in 'bad' marriages	Tenuous intimacy as fantasies about others increase	Intimacy is threatened by ageing and by boredom vis-à-vis a secure and stable relationship: departure of children may increase or decrease intimacy	Struggle to maintain intimacy in the face of eventual separation: in most marriages this dimension achieves a stable plateau
Establishment of definite patterns of decision making and dominance	Power in outside world is tested vis-à-vis power in the marriage	Conflicts often increase when children leave, and security appears threatened	Survival fears stir up needs for control and dominance
Nuclear family closes boundaries	Disruption due to re-evaluation: drive versus restabilization	Boundaries are usually fixed except in crises such as illness, death, job change, and sudden shift in role relation-ships	Loss of family and friends leads to closing in of boundaries: physical envir-onment is crucial in maintaining ties with the outside world

Begin to become aware of our personal histories. Part of becoming an adult is the need to differentiate ourselves from our families of origin with their shared myths and phantasies, their collusions and their need for us to play assigned roles within the family drama. For many of us, becoming an adult involves not merely leaving the family home and putting distance between ourselves and those who remain, but also in freeing ourselves from the expectations and myths which have been central to our lives since childhood.

Integration of our developing sexual experience, including both heterosexual and homosexual experience, and begin to learn the capacity for intimacy with a partner. Nowadays, with the far earlier onset of sexual potency and the adolescent push towards early sexual experience, this has become a shared task between adolescence and early adulthood. It is one which many people find far more testing than in the recent past, when it was possible to work out such problems with the help of courtship rituals and long engagements, which no longer seem acceptable today. The enormous emphasis which we put upon sexual experience and behaviour at all levels of our society, the emergence of new philosophies of personal freedom for male and female homosexuals and the rise of feminism all present the young adult of today with a far more complex developmental task than that faced by his forebears. The latter could seemingly afford to take things more slowly, and were in part protected from many of the questions which face the young of today by an unquestioning acceptance of religious and ethical norms. It has to be said that the revolution in sexual mores which began – according to Western myth – in the 'Swinging Sixties' has complicated this search for sexual self-identification in a way that those who preached sexual freedom in the wake of the Pill and Penicillin certainly never contemplated. It needs no great sociological skill or knowledge on my part to set out how first the movement towards sexual freedom and then the capacity to be genuinely free of the fear of unwanted pregnancy led to an increased promiscuity, which in its turn has now been compromised by the fear of sexually transmitted diseases, in particular the fear of HIV and AIDS. This phase of young adult life has become one of the major preoccupations of our times, and is, in my view, very taxing for the young person of today.

In the context of this changed attitude towards both sexuality and intimacy, the whole question of marriage or partnership in Western society must be addressed. Choice of a partner has become far more complex. The pressure to marry and have children seems to have a different series of determinants than before. With the breakdown of religious, legal and social constraints on the actual condition of marriage, the range of choices for the young adult is clearly far greater. Indeed, the question often arises whether to bother with a marriage ceremony at all, or to settle for a series of more or less stable cohabitations, with or without children.

Whether or not to become a parent. I have worked with a number of young women in their late 20s and early 30s for whom this was a central theme in their self-questioning. On the one hand they had very strong unconscious expectations of becoming a mother and completing their Oedipal struggle by having a child of their own, and in that way becoming at last the potent adult they had always felt themselves capable of being. On the other hand, even where there was a man with whom they could set up a reasonable and supportive family life, and who would provide them with what Winnicott called a facilitating environment – which may more or less chime with the kind of expectations which their early life in their families of origin has led them to expect – they find themselves in conflict with another part of their inner worlds which has led them to perceive that success in a given career is perhaps of equal importance to their narcissistic needs and feeling of their own identity. The conflict then centres around whether to put their careers on hold at what may well be a vital stage in terms of promotion or other achievements in order to have children. This may be done because the biological clock is winding down and they have to use their childbearing years before it is too late for them to meet the conscious and unconscious needs which are driving them towards parenthood.

Forging a personal work identity and making decisions about a personal career. The choice of career and the stability of the work environment have become far more variable during the last 20 years. While it was once possible for a young adult to consult with their parents, teachers and mentors before making a decision, and expect that this would represent their life choice, such commitments have now become rare, while the possibility of a stable career is often just not on offer. There are a far greater variety of university courses available, while at the same time career prospects have become far more vague. This places a far greater strain on the individual, and makes far greater demands on their relationships to both their actual families and their internal security as well.

For those not fortunate enough to have clear vocational goals in the way that an aspiring veterinary surgeon might, the pressure is far greater. The stated goal of the present Government is for one in three young people to go to University, even though they are reluctant to supply enough places to meet the demand that already exists, the gulf between those fortunate enough to have achieved some form of tertiary education and those who do not have the good fortune to actually get there is becoming greater and greater. It is perhaps no accident that there is a proliferation of crime among the young, and that those who do not have access to further education, despite its drawbacks are finding themselves gradually downgraded. For the young people of today, once again the task is complicated by the loss of the ethical and religious norms of behaviour which did so much to stabilize society in former times.

Settling Down

In the face of these problems, ageing is at first only a minor irritant – something which happens to other people and which in no way impinges on ourselves and our existential needs and wishes. But as we reach the period of the just-noticeable difference, when in the mid-30s the body begins to betray us and fail by small increments, when the passage of time is perceived as having an effect upon us, then we at last become aware of the processes of ageing.

By the 30s, the ordinary young adult will begin to have become aware of and begun the process of coming to terms with his or her condition, and to have made a number of commitments. He or she will probably have found what seems a reasonably stable work or profession, will have settled into a committed sexual relationship with a long-term partner, and have become aware of and started to pursue long-term goals in both the professional and the personal sphere. In many cases people will have started families and committed themselves to the long-term welfare of one or more children.

In a way, the decade between 30 and 40 is when people conform most closely to social norms and the demands of their internal parents: they either feel they are succeeding in meeting those demands, or begin to become more and more dissatisfied with the situation they have created for themselves. In this phase both we and those close to us are closely examined in terms of the ideal and critical aspects of the super-ego, the parental part of our internal value system.

This phase can often provoke considerable conflict between partners, when, in the aftermath of having children, the underlying dissonance which each partner brings to marriage and parenthood gradually becomes apparent. As personal agendas diverge, so conflict comes to the fore. Often the female wants more time spent on the partnership and the well-being of the family, which has become her primary task. They also embody the expectations which women bring from their childhoods, and the actualization of their internal worlds. Their partners, on the other hand, are more and more committed to their work and worldly success, which will often meet their needs of response to the relationship and rivalry with the fathers of their early childhoods.

The mid-30s are the times when longer-range goals take over and the immediacies of the post-adolescent period begin to fall away. Firm friendships of a new kind begin to be made, sometimes on the basis of shared ideals and beliefs, but more often on the basis of early infantile relationships. Goals become more subtle. People begin to be more at ease with themselves, and to truly develop their executive and creative capacities. For many of us there is a decrease in the neurotic acting out of the adolescent and post-adolescent period, which is replaced by a firmer understanding of who and what we are as we move into middle adulthood. Perhaps most of all, for many of us the demands of the inner world are for a while muted and we can feel that we are our own men and women.

From the point of view of the dynamic psychotherapist, this is the time when the long-term effects of childhood experience begin to become infused with the actualities of parenthood and work experience. In some ways it is still a moot point whether our behaviour remains dominated by the long-lasting effects of our Oedipal experience, or whether the actual creation of a new family overlays and in some way replaces our earlier phantasies and expectations of what we think might happen to us. My own view is that there is a dynamic combination of the two experiences, although it has to be said that under stress there may be a regression to earlier ways of dealing with matters. I am thinking here of Mr A., a man in his late 30s.

Mr A. had made a good second marriage to a woman who he felt was a nearly ideal partner in most aspects of their lives. His new wife had brought with her to this marriage – which was also a second marriage for her – two young children. While Mr A. was on fairly good terms with his stepchildren, he found he became absolutely overcome with rage when his wife would insist they take the children away on weekends with them. At such times Mr A. found himself almost physically attacking his wife and behaving very badly towards the children, whom he ordinarily found to be reasonably tolerable and pleasant people. When we worked on this in his therapy, it became clear that this response – which Mr A. felt to be quite alien to his normal tolerant adult self – was related to early experiences of abandonment by his mother, who had repeatedly left him in his early years. His wife had taken the place of the much-desired and idealized maternal figure. When she 'left' Mr A. by insisting on taking the children with them, and not letting him have her entirely to himself as he wished in Oedipal terms, he responded not in an adult way, but with infantile rage.

Ideally, during this decade a new family unit is produced, with its own rules and behaviours, attributions of power and responsibilities, and reworking of the constant themes of love and work. Each partner takes up and reworks their internal world and its conflicts in relationship to the other, with the children acting in terms of each partner's expectations and phantasies about how their partner should be and how they should behave. This means that every family carries with it an entire series of dynamics which are generated by both the internal worlds of the parents and the interaction between these, and the response of the children.

We are born into incredibly complex family organizations and expectations. It is my view that the decade from 30 to 40 is the one which above all is devoted to the establishment and working out of these multifarious patterns. Many of my friends now in their late 50s and early 60s say these are the years which the locusts ate:

looking back on them they have no real recollection of the period, perhaps because they were forced to live them so vividly that they had almost no time to reflect on the process which was occurring both within them and around them.

The developmental tasks of this decade include the establishment of acceptable ways of decision-making, and dominance within the family sphere. This is the time of the establishment of the nuclear family with all its merits and defaults. If things go well, this is also the time of increasing intimacy and trust between the partners, which may well lay the foundations for good experiences as they age and begin to have to face the tasks which await them in the second half of their lives.

Mid-Life Transition

Somewhere around the age of 40, all sorts of stresses begin to impinge on the individual. In particular he or she has to come to grips with the question of whether they have achieved the sort of success which may have caused them to make an enormous investment. It is not at all uncommon for therapists to meet people who are suffering from the 'Nobel Prize syndrome' – the realization that they are never going to achieve a hoped-for, long-awaited and phantasied success. Whatever one does, the professional chair or the longed for partnership is not coming our way, nor will we have much chance of finding Prince (or Princess) Charming on the doorstep complete with glass slipper. For women who have not yet made the long-term relationship they have desired, the chance of motherhood will be slipping away as the biological clock winds down. Both sexes have to take a long, cool look at their lives and what they have achieved and come to terms with their failures, both in terms of internal reality and in terms of their ambitions and relationships. A dentist of my acquaintance said to me at the age of 38, 'There was this kid of 18 who decided he wanted to become a dentist because his dad told him he'd always make a decent living that way. Here I am at 38 and I'm stuck with his choice. If I had it to do now, I certainly wouldn't make the same one.'

At this time of life there is a great efflorescence of anxiety and disquiet in people about where they are in their lives and what they have actually achieved. Sometimes, as in the case of Ms R., this means a change of careers, which may involve an enormous sacrifice for themselves and for those close to them:

> Ms R. was a woman of considerable artistic gifts who had always felt enormously put upon by her very narrow-minded and domineering mother. She therefore had very little in the way of self-esteem and appropriate narcissism. Although Ms R. was extremely attractive and was constantly pursued by young men while at university, she only remembered the one occasion her mother had told her that her breasts were too large. Ever since that time she had regarded herself as unattractive. The result was that Ms R. began to act out with older men, who would reassure her of her attractiveness and be the loving and attentive fathers that her own father had not been able to be.
>
> Rather than pursuing the artistic career for which she was well fitted, Ms R. had suddenly decided to study medicine, and had qualified as a doctor. She felt that in this way she could identify herself as a person who was not dependent on her mother's way of looking at life. She followed this career until she was 38, when she became extremely depressed. She decided to give up medicine and pursue a career in which she could identify herself not in opposition to her mother, but as a person in her own right. We were able to work out her difficulties with her identity and its infantile roots. Ms R. retrained as a journalist in a country where she is physically as far from her mother as she can be.

While Ms R. is far happier now than she would have been had she continued as a disgruntled and unhappy doctor, such changes can bring all sorts of problems in their wake. While many people use what they have learned of life from 20 to 35 to help them make a more appropriate second career choice, they are always up against those who have been doing the job at least for a decade. Generally speaking, they therefore start with an enormous disadvantage compared to their contemporaries. In some careers of course this does not matter: a man who discovers a vocation for the priesthood after 15 years working in a large business may bring knowledge of the world to his new work and colleagues. However, as we see only too often in those who decide they wish to help the sufferings of others by becoming, for example, psychotherapists – and in that way treating their own difficulties through their patients – the gap between idealization of their new profession and their skills as professionals, no matter how hard or intensively they train, is far too great.

This is not only true of my own profession, but those of many other disciplines as well. I recall one patient who had had the good fortune to receive a large inheritance and had given up his job as a buyer for a large company to train as a barrister – a role he had always fantasized should have been his had his family not insisted he have a secure job. He was successful in passing the examinations only to find he had great difficulty in finding a chambers which would take him in spite of his business experience, or solicitors who would send him cases to plead in court. For this person this response to the normal transitional phase was the wrong one, and his attempt to bring his fantasy to life was not appropriate.

Figure 1 also points out a very important source of conflict in families which is linked with the theme of ageing. Individuals age in terms of a whole series of differential time scales. We live in simultaneous and different scales – physical, emotional, relational, historical, and so on – and this is very true of partners also. A well-known scenario is that in which the man is faced with a partner who, now that the children are able to be more independent, wishes either to return to a career which she has laid aside for the sake of their mutual children, or to explore new possibilities. Many men find it very difficult to tolerate the new-found independence of their partner, and prefer to remain in a situation in which they have a dependent woman who does not appear as a threat. They may find ways of abandoning their partner and families, taking up with a new, younger woman. She will become for them the dependent, non-threatening female who enables them to remain safely in their role as the dominant, much-needed male. This is very difficult for the woman who is just beginning to make a stab at personal freedom, since she often gets left with the children of the first marriage, who inevitably act as a brake on what she is seeking, as well as the possibility of finding a new and acceptable male partner.

This dependency scenario has a great part to play in the number of separations which seem to peak at this age. There is also a very important unconscious sexual factor which comes into play as well during this time.

A very marked awareness of the diminution in physiological potency particularly affects men in their late 30s and early 40s. This drives them back both on fears of impotence and on their fantasies, which have often been formed in adolescence as a defence against the fear of castration by older and more potent males. The possession of a young, nubile – and therefore desirable – woman is seen as being a reassurance against fears of not being able to measure up against other, more dominant, male rivals. The infantile roots of such castration anxiety are not difficult to discern; it will depend on the individual male and his sexual history whether or not he needs the additional reassurance of a new, younger woman to bolster his fear of his potential impotence.

This is above all the time when sexual fantasies return, and with them the need for a woman who, whether in terms of infantile perversions or in the conquest of a new and desirable sexual partner, can be endowed with many of the characteristics with which the familiar sexual partner can no longer be credited.

I remember one patient who discovered that her husband of 20 years had recently taken to visiting prostitutes. She had the courage to seek out some of the women and try to find out what her very inhibited husband was seeking from them. She said to me, 'I went out and got a few sexual aids thinking that I could give him what he wanted far better than those women'. But she was disappointed: it was not just a question of sexual frustration in the marriage, but the return of a whole perverse system which had been repressed for many years and which her husband could only allow himself to act on with prostitutes. As you might expect, her failure led her elsewhere and she found a new and less-inhibited man with whom she was able to have a freer and richer relationship.

Middle Adulthood

We can consider this phase as beginning in the mid-40s and continuing until the end of the 50s. In many ways it is a rich and rewarding time of life for many people. Even in these youth-oriented times, the person may reach positions of strength and responsibility, with the rewards which accompany such achievements. Stability and success go a long way towards helping resolve the Oedipal problems which beset men in particular, and many feel that at long last they can lay the family ghosts to rest, so that Hamlet's father's ghost no longer needs to stalk the battlements at night.

At the same time, the developing family is beginning to consolidate as the children in their turn pass through adolescence and make their own play for individuality and freedom. For many adults this offers the chance to rework their own conflicts by giving their children the freedom of which they themselves felt deprived, while their own unconscious conflicts may be re-fought but on different battlefields. However this may work out, there is often a greater sense of inner security and safety as the new situation unwinds. Where the children's independence is not too traumatic, both parents can welcome the phenomenon of the empty nest, and rejoice in their children's achievements.

Long-cherished projects which have been put aside because of the demands of family and their economic, social and psychological needs can be taken up and explored; this often comes as the antidote to the increasing boredom that familiarity and the absorption in the parental task brings into the marriage. It may come as a lifesaver when one or the other partner absorbs themselves in some new task or activity which had been impossible before. It may be that the long-awaited opportunity turns out to be a disappointment and the reality far less rewarding than the long-held dream might have suggested. However, as they are now mature adults, the possibility of taking on a new task is planned for and thought through, often far more carefully than it would have been when they were younger.

This is also a time when conflicts can no longer be dealt with so easily by fight-flight mechanisms. Instead of being able to pick up and go off to another city or country; instead of being able to change jobs or career paths; instead of being able to find another partner, men and women at this age are struggling with the successes of structures and relationships which they have constructed over perhaps one or two decades. Under these circumstances, and with the increasing awareness of intellectual and particularly physical deficit which now begins, the trend is much more towards the psychosomatic and psychological expression of conflict. (The enormous quantity of tranquillizers which have been ingested in the past 20 or so years bears witness to the inadequacy of our response to these problems.)

Anxiety and depression now come to the fore, as do the

psychosomatic manifestations with which we are all familiar. A bad back; a difficult menopause; irritable bowel syndrome; a virus which persists for years and gives rise to all sorts of manifestations which prevent the individual from being the person they would otherwise be; all these are familiar problems in the GP's surgery. It is here that the theorists of psychotherapy and psychoanalysis, with their very infant and young-person-centred culture, have to bear some of the blame. Proper counselling and therapy, even if applied in a very brief format, can do a great deal to help those who wish to change and to move forward in their lives in a constructive and creative fashion.

However, it does not do to define ageing as a negative process, which is better understood and defined as a positive process for many people. The period of middle adulthood is a very productive time during which people can with luck and forethought begin to produce their best work. Psychologically it is a time when good relationships grow and deepen, and friendships become even more important than they were in earlier life. People can prepare themselves for the vicissitudes of the Third Age, which is now looming over the horizon; lessons can be learned from older colleagues and friends and their ways of dealing with this challenge.

The Young-Old

With the arrival at age 60, we can begin to discuss later life. The dread words 'old age' now begin to form part of our everyday vocabulary. The infinitely preferable term Third Age – third being after childhood and parenthood – seems to me well worth making, enabling us to take a more positive view of ageing.

At somewhere around 60, the question of our own personal survival begins to emerge. We should distinguish sharply here between those whose lives have been defined to a greater or lesser extent by their work roles, and those for whom the release from the work arena will come as a blessed relief.

The threat of retirement and ill health is far greater for those who do not have the personal resources – whether financial or psychological – to plan for their retirement, and feel that it will represent a loss of what has defined them and their entitlement to respect in society.

The challenges are also ongoing: it is hard to maintain the interest and excitement necessary to keep oneself fit as one ages, let alone improve one's standards. All the problems of an ageing body and the demands one places on it are gradually, and then more frequently, brought to the foreground.

This process of reconciling the past, the present and the future is one of the main tasks of ageing, particularly as we enter the era of the 'young-old' – those who are still in reasonable health and intellectually unimpaired.

These are the times when we have to come to terms with profound personal conflicts which have been with us since infancy, and which may have been submerged during our early and middle adulthood years. We have to cope with our changing sexual needs and attitudes; the change from a sexuality which is hormonally driven to one which depends more and more on intimacy and loving kindness in the face of changing physical capacities. This naturally brings for men a revival of early Oedipal and castration phantasies and their concomitant anxieties. For women, the change from physical potency and the capacity to bear children to post-menopausal sexuality inevitably brings once more into focus the question of their relationships to their children and to their own mothers.

As I write, a controversy has arisen over a woman of 62 who is expecting her first child and the implications of such surgical techniques for all involved. I remember one lady who came to me at the age of 76. She wanted me to help her to mourn her lifelong attachment to her dominant father. This had caused her to abort her children, which had left her – despite many real achievements – feeling that in the most vital of all ways she had been a failure, since she had never produced the children whom she now so desperately desired to give her meaning in her old age. There was of course nothing I could do to make good her loss, but I was able to give her a place where she could express what she herself called her 'madness', and be, not her ordinary successful and highly respected self, but a grieving little girl who was wounded to the very heart.

Many of us as adults still have to deal with problems of separation and individuation from our early childhood. In a very real sense we have to rework the problems which we faced in our early lives about being alone, and how to be ourselves in terms of internal environments which will have both changed and grown during our lives, but which paradoxically are now offering us the same problems once again.

Those who have been able to use their early environments in what Donald Winnicott would have called a 'facilitating way' can come to terms with the challenges that ageing produces in a productive way. The old person who wishes to live in his or her own home, which, while often inconvenient, is known and familiar, rather than to be pushed into some retirement community is probably far healthier psychologically than the person who succumbs to their children's wishes and allows themselves to be parked in physical security but in psychological peril. It is the latter who go into terminal decline and quickly die when put in a place of 'safety'.

Old people, like young children, can be alone with themselves if they have developed the appropriate internal resources, and can create a satisfying and worthwhile life for themselves. I remember one old lady, Mrs R., who came to see me every week at the clinic for seven years after her 88th birthday. I quickly helped her with her fears of death and desertion, but it then became clear that Mrs R. needed contact with an institution to enable her to maintain herself in her little flat where she lived alone. She had no living relatives, and made little call on the statutory services. We often talked of her going into some sort of protected housing, but she felt that as long as she could come and see me for a half an hour a week and talk to the receptionists – who were genuinely fond of her and would give her a cup of tea and let her tell them about the television programmes which she had been watching – she could very well manage on her own. Although some of my colleagues complained that it was very expensive that she should be given half an hour of consultant time a week, on any actuarial scale of values this was a relatively cheap alternative to supporting her in a home. Mrs R. managed very well on her own with the minimal support that she was given, and was, I think, far happier than she would otherwise have been.

The young-old are those who can accept the developmental tasks of ageing and accomplish the late adult transition with grace and not too much pain. It must be hard for some of us to accept that we have to give up positions of power and responsibility, but it may be that in doing so we are freeing ourselves for a different style of living that is equally rewarding. In many Eastern cultures late life is regarded as a period when men are freed from the challenges of everyday life and may spend their time working out their relationships to God and the universe.

Many of us are not perhaps so lucky, given that Western culture is more focused on activity than contemplation. Nevertheless, we will have to find acceptable roles for ourselves in late age, and live and work through the problems of a failing body and changing relationships. All the fears of childhood can re-emerge, which may be exacerbated by the way in which our own relatives are encouraged by the culture to place us in the relatively non-threatening patient or child role. Where older people agree to accept these roles, they quickly lose their independence of mind and body and begin to deteriorate.

The decrements of old age have to be faced openly. We all have to live through the loss of friends, partners and, worst of all, the children who should have been immortal and carried the best parts of us. It is here, paradoxically, that the psychotherapists with their experience of helping people to accept and rework chagrin, pain and loss have a great deal to contribute – but perhaps because it may be too close to home for many of them they do not do so. When people go to the University of the Third Age and audit courses in foreign languages, or take up pottery with verve and enthusiasm in their 70s, these are life-enhancing activities which are not hypomanic but rather age-appropriate, and deserve the understanding and recognition they do not necessarily receive in our present culture.

This period of young-oldness can last for many years. I recently attended a meeting at which Enid Balint gave a paper to the Psychoanalytic Society to celebrate her 90th birthday, and got much the best of the discussion. One of those attending was 93, and told me that she was writing her eighth book.

If one can achieve the independence of spirit which is essential, then I can see no reason other than the inevitable physical deterioration which time brings why this should not be one of the most enjoyable and rewarding periods of people's lives. Death and taxes are inevitable for us all, but I think the motto for those who have achieved the late-life transition with all its challenges is 'We owe death a life.'

2
Sexuality

During the last century we have experienced a quantum jump in life expectancy in the West. Until 1850 life expectancy for the average English woman might be somewhere between 40 to 45 years, while men might live from 45 to 50 years. Women reached sexual maturity later than the young women of today; there was a very high incidence of deaths in childbirth or as the result of multiple pregnancies, thus a much smaller proportion of women survived to enjoy a post-menopausal sexual life. Recent studies suggest that until the end of the nineteenth century no more than eight per cent of the population survived the age of 60.

After the turn of the century, however, matters changed dramatically. The proportion of the older population has been completely transformed in this century.

Masters and Johnson in their magisterial study of human sexuality say:

> Women beyond the age of 50 have usually resolved most of the problems associated with raising a family. Once the exhaustive physical and extensive mental demands of brood protection have been obviated by the maturation of the family group, it is only natural that new directions are sought as outlets for unexpended mental energy and reawakened mental activity. Thus a significant increase in sexual activity marks the revived sex drive of these middle-aged women. We suggest that a woman who has had a happy, well-adjusted and stimulating marriage may progress through the menopause and post-menopausal years with little or no interruption in the frequency of or interest in sexual activity.[7]

On the other hand, Masters and Johnson also warn that:

> There is an increasingly large proportion of the female population that is diametrically opposite to the reasonably adjusted individual described above. Such women use the excuse of their advancing years in order to avoid the

embarrassment of inadequate personal performance or the frustrations of unresolved sexual tensions.

In their view, the Victorian concept that the older woman should have no innate interest in any form of sexual activity, and that post-menopausal women naturally lose their sexual drive probably has arisen from the same source. Even dreams or fantasies with sexual content are rejected in the widespread popular belief that sexual intercourse is an unsuitable and improper indulgence for any woman of or beyond middle age.

The same is true of men. Here Masters and Johnson question the popular belief that sexual responsiveness wanes in the human male as he ages. They note that a major difference exists between the response patterns of the male aged 41 to 60 years and those past 60. In the latter, the difference is marked by loss of maintained locus of sexual tension and reduced reactive intensity during sexual expression. Not only does coital activity usually decrease, but the incidence of masturbation and nocturnal emission also is slowed with the advancing years.

Nevertheless, the maintenance of an enjoyable sexual life is based upon consistency of active sexual expression. Provided that older men have active sexual partners who are interested in sexual performance, there is little needed to support sexual adequacy in a 70-or even 80-year-old man. The factors which militate against adequate sexual expression in the ageing male are fatigue, physiological and physical decline, tension, stress, alcohol and lack of interest in the partner. There is also an obviously accumulative deficit to do with fear of impotence, which can be activated by one or more failures. Masters and Johnson record that all their male subjects feared impotence after the age of 40 despite the fact that they might never have suffered any such problems at any time in their lives.

Nevertheless, Masters and Johnson feel that regularity of sexual intercourse, with adequate physical well-being and healthy mental orientation in the ageing process will combine to provide a sexually stimulating climate within a relationship. This will in turn decrease sexual tension and provide a capacity for sexual performance which frequently may extend beyond 80 years.

So far the facts are quite clear: provided they have appropriate stimulation, both sexes can look forward to a healthy sexual life well into their late 70s at least, or until the time of major senile decrement. But while the facts have been clearly established by modern research it seems that psychologically most of us find this hard to accept – the possibility of a satisfying and rewarding sexuality in later life is not generally recognized or provided for.

It may still be regarded as voyeuristic, even in our relatively relaxed times, to talk to older people about their sexual lives. When I was training young psychotherapists, I discovered they often had difficulty speaking with older patients about their sexual experiences – difficulties they would not have encountered with their contemporaries. For one therapist it was hard to take a sexual history from a 70-year-old woman who cheerfully told the interviewer of her ongoing sexual activity, perhaps with several men, or of her continued masturbation and her masturbation fantasies.

In our culture, those past the conventional age of reproduction are somehow supposed to have become asexual. Homes for the aged separate them and treat them as if they were prepubescent children, perhaps to defend the staff against confrontation with the fact of the ongoing sexuality of the elders and all that it stands for. We have not got around to coping with the true facts of (later) life.

Recent research in the area has not helped a great deal. On the whole such studies as there are are restricted to white middle-class populations. The authors tend to neglect the possibility that the elderly are interested in and therefore capable of an engagement in sexual activity outside the bounds of matrimony. The authors tend to measure certain correlates of sexual activity, rather than looking at the relationships involved. Gaarza and Dresel suggest that there are several important areas to look at. They find that there are gradual declines in sexual activity, interest and quality and that these factors continue into the later years of marriage. This was particularly so for females and for the older research subjects. Elderly husbands and wives are generally aware of such declines and assign different interpretations to them. However, there is some evidence that slight increases in sexual activity occur for older persons, largely resulting from structural changes (such as the empty nest) or redefinitions regarding the marital partner and the meaning of marriage.

It is worth noting that responsibility for declining sexual activity is directed unequivocally to the husbands. Husbands typically blame themselves for declines in sexual activity and wives typically blame husbands. Compensatory forms of intimacy might emerge as stabilizing factors in some elderly marriages.

It is worth noting, too, that the relationship between religion and sexual expression has been largely ignored. However, the few pieces of available research on the elderly support what is known about sexual expression among younger age groups. Specifically, religious devotion is inversely correlated to sexual frequency: further, devoutness mitigates the effect of sexual performance on marital satisfaction.

I should add that other major factors such as income, race, education and social class have largely escaped inquiry. Certainly, I know of no consistent findings in this area.

What is striking is that without exception present levels of sex drive are directly related to sexual drive in the young. Researchers do not enquire into the impact of sexual activity on the happiness of the marriage: in one study all respondents over the age of 70 considered that their marriages were happy, but only half were sexually active. It is possible that if cessation of sexual intercourse has the potential of lowering overall marital satisfaction, it can be compensated for by other forms of sexual expression. If married happiness in later life is not dependent on frequency of inter-course, it must be dependent on something else, or at least highly correlated with that something else. My own answer lies in the term 'intimacy'. In older people, various sexual behaviours merge together to produce an exchange far richer than in the young person.

Among healthy, active older adults, the normal decline in male sexual drive results in a greater valuation of more diffuse forms of sexuality; greater tolerance; a capacity, as in homosexual couples, to be more attentive to and responsive to their partner's needs, particularly in terms of partial sexual drives and personal perfor-mance; and the possibility of a more diffuse but equally psycho-logically fulfilling sexual response. The refusal to accept these ways of looking at sexual behaviours could easily lead to a 'new ageism'. One authority suggests that if we refuse to accept this view then we are liable to see 'older people who respond to their inner worlds or enjoy and desire passive entertainment as challenges to be overcome, rather than as individuals who are adapting to a lifelong or recent preference that could only be realized fully when retirement and the empty nest made it possible.'

This view confirms those of David Guttman, to whose work I referred in the previous chapter. He has convincingly demonstrated that in the post-parental period there is a re-emergence of the gender identities of both sexes which have had to be suppressed during parenthood. Men can now begin to explore the more feminine, passive sides of their natures, and can turn to all sorts of activities which have been suppressed by the need to be operative in order to support a family and take the paternal role. Similarly, women can become more active, operational, and more readily take initiatives. It is likely that this is true of sexual roles as well, and that such partial forms of sexual activity as oral sex, mutual masturbation, and the exploration of skin erotism will become more acceptable and more satisfying to both partners.

There are other ways, too, in which late-life sexuality differs from earlier phases of adulthood. The earlier tendency towards serial monogamy, after the trial periods of the teens and 20s, is not so appropriate for the older adult. I have worked with a considerable number of patients who have been married for 30 to 40 years where there is a tacit or open understanding, or some form of collusion has been arrived at, so that one partner will seek sexual satisfaction in a stable extramarital relationship with a third party. This has the effect of preserving or underpinning relationships which could otherwise have lost meaning after the departure of the children.

There is also the question of psychological safety, and how to come to terms with the narcissistic losses of cherished aspects of the self, or the failure of a lifelong sexualized defence against anxiety. In some cases which I recall, men who have been impotent pretty well all their adult lives have come to therapy in the hope of changing their sexual behaviour so that they can take advantage of the possibilities which new relationships with kind and loving women were offering them. Yet almost always this turned out to be impossible. The reason has been that they have been unable to change because of their need to keep women, sexuality and children at bay. As Kingsley Amis portrays in his novel *Jake's Thing*, there comes a time when the establishment of a sense of personal safety is more important than the fulfilment of sexual wishes, no matter how dominant and driving these men may have been in earlier years.

It might help to understand if I relate the story of Ms C., whom I have known vaguely for some 20 years.

An artist and a writer, Ms C. married a sculptor from the Mediterranean, and had four children by him. Some years ago she was happy to retire from her professional work and took up an artistic pursuit. She was referred because she was very overweight and could not manage to stick to a given diet.

The colleague who sent her to me said that she 'is a handsome lady of 68, with elegantly coiffured hair, but she carries herself with grace and is quite sexually attractive. She betrays some tension in the way that she sits and moves restlessly, but she talks well and indeed pours out her words as if under pressure to communicate. She uses the interview well, and is responsive to interpretation or explorations of sensitive areas.'

Ms C. came because she wanted help with her craving for sweet food, which she has had all her life. She was a fat baby, large at birth, whose mother was not able to breast-feed her. After a miserable time on milk substitutes, she was eventually put on cow's milk, on which she thrived so that she weighed about two stones when she was one year old. Ms C. has always been fat, and has tried many ways of controlling her diet, but in fact she hates having to.

Ms C. basically does not want to eat. She has never known what it is to be hungry and she does not like most food. What she does is to eat too much of the foods she has a liking for, which are largely sweet foods, to which she is addicted and becomes very bad tempered if she is deprived of them. She is like an alcoholic in that she will hide foods in places where she can later find them in case she runs out. She lost four stone when she went on a Weight Watchers' diet: she felt marvellous, liked her body, but felt that she had much less of a presence, and that she was less significant as a person. She recognizes that she needs to be big, and that she has a need always to have something in her mouth.

Ms C. did not see herself as having any other significant problems. She perceived herself as a happy person, who had had an interesting and rewarding life, and who could now enjoy her retirement. When I first began to work with her she was having an affair which was very rewarding sexually, and which had done a great deal to bolster her self-confidence. Financially she was reasonably secure. However, it was not difficult for us to get to the underlying insecurity about herself. All her life she had had a sense of inferiority about her appearance, her personality and her intelligence so that she has had to put herself over to people in such a way as to placate them, please them or to act in a manner which she believed they would find acceptable. Sexuality has always been an enormous consolation for her. She considered herself to have been a fat, unattractive young woman, but even then she knew that she could give off a great aura of sexuality, and became quite promiscuous, although only in a masturbatory manner.

However, when she eventually married a very intellectually distinguished Italian, which constituted a great smack in the face for her very snobbish English upper-middle-class family, she was not able to consummate the marriage for over two years because of an acute vaginismus. Unfortunately, the marriage later went on the rocks, largely because of the eccentricities of her husband. She described going through another very promiscuous period in her late 40s and early 50s when sexuality was again a great consolation to her – it became something which 'sweetened' her life.

There are clear connections between her image of herself and the representation of her mother. Ms C.'s mother was perceived by her, and to a large extent probably was, a vain egocentric, attractive woman with a considerable personality, who was jealous of people who received more attention than herself. It is clear that she could not bring up her daughter to feel confident in her appearance, her personality, and, as so often with such women, especially her sexuality. Ms C. felt that her mother's view on sexuality was that it really was something that should not exist – although she suspected a double standard and that her mother actually had some extramarital affairs.

Apart from her painful early-feeding history. Ms C. had been an evidently unhappy child until the arrival of a new governess at the age of four. This governess stayed with her until she was 14, and turned out to be a very sweet person whom she idealized. Ms C. realized that she had used this governess as a model and a controlling force throughout her life; she still did not do the things that her governess would have said were 'not nice'.

The other side of Ms C. – the screaming child – was linked to what she called the 'nasty side' of herself. She could count on the fingers of one hand the number of times when she had lost her temper, and when she had become so violent as almost to be murderous. There was one dreadful occasion when she attacked one of her sons, who was then about 14 years old, who was wearing a bandage over a minor injury to his eye: he wished to remove the bandage, since he felt that his friends would mock him. Ms C. attacked him violently, both physically and emotionally, and he actually ran away from home because she told him she no longer wished to see him.

In a more controlled form, her 'nastiness' came out in her wish to attract men, to entice them sexually and then to reject them. Being aware of this side of herself, she usually managed to control and contain it.

Ms C.'s dreams were interesting: she was always looking for a house to sell or to buy, but there was always something wrong – it was always too big or too small or something was not right. When we discussed the dreams it seemed clear that this house could well represent her self and her view of her own body – when I said to her that this is the self in which she has never really enjoyed living, she began to weep.

I worked with Ms C. for about a year; in our contract we had agreed that we would try and get behind her symptoms and try to deal with aspects of herself that she found unacceptable, such as the 'nasty', screaming part of her that lay behind the pleasant façade. It was clear that this would also involve looking at her idealizations and the tensions involved with the splitting of her mother and her governess.

About a year after the therapy began, Ms C.'s daughter, with whom she had always been very close, telephoned to say that she had just learned that her next eldest brother, Ms C.'s third child, had committed suicide. I offered to see her the next day, and she came to my room accompanied by her daughter, and asked me to kiss her. 'All my men are doing that', she said. She then poured out her grief and loss and anger at the loss of her son, who was in many ways her favourite child. The ostensible reason for his suicide was trivial, although it seemed far more likely that the reason was that he had had a psychotic episode brought on by a broken love affair. After this, I increased her sessions to twice a week and we worked as best as we could on her depression, grief and rage.

Ms C. was surprised by the extent and amount of sympathy she received from her son's friends, and was extremely grateful to them for all that they did for her. She busied herself in organizing a memorial service at the local church, which was well attended and therefore gratifying for her remaining children and for herself. With time she worked through something of her rage and her depression, and eventually regained something of her old, well-defended personality. She kept on with her creative work, continued her love affair and seemed to be well in control of her life. She said to me later, 'My daughter says that she feels things much more vividly since her brother's death. I suppose that I do too, but not in the same way. I feel them and suddenly I am aware that he is not there. It's not a help as it is for her. I feel things, but it is not the same any more.' The wound is too great.

The point that I wish to emphasize, however, is that for Ms C. the sexual relationship with her lover was of extreme importance. While at times she was very resentful of the fact that he came to see her with the knowledge, and I suspect the compliance, of his wife, who like him is 75 years old, they continued to have a good, ongoing sexual relationship, which represented for Ms C. an ongoing sexual response to herself and her circumstances, which have been crucial to her survival as a person and her feeling of worth in herself.

There were of course times when she did not wish to make love, and then she would tell him this quite openly; on the other hand when she had a success in a creative endeavour, which represented a considerable success for a woman who was by now in her 70s, she was delighted when he came the next day and they could celebrate by going to bed together. She said to me 'Really, I never in my life remember it being so good. I really felt that I was loved, wanted and cheered. It was a celebration.' I think that most of us would sympathize with this feeling, and I was very touched to realize that for Ms C., her continuing sexual activity enabled her to realize important creative aspects of herself in a way which I considered highly appropriate.

Of course, Ms C. continued to have major problems, and I am sure she never recovered from the death of her son – although she seemed to have found a marvellous compromise solution by refusing to accept that he was dead and carrying on conversations with him in her mind, while at the same time acknowledging that this was not the case. But in all this there was an aspect of her body which could feel valued, which could respond to a man, which she could feel to be worthwhile and satisfying in a way which it was not in earlier parts of her life. Her ongoing sexual activity did a great deal to preserve her from depression and from falling into utter despair. In her case, later life sexuality had become a lifeline, without which I think that she might well have become depressed, morose and liable to fall into psychosomatic illnesses from which she would not easily have recovered.

A patient for whom late-life sexuality presented a rather different problem was Mr T. When I first met him he was 61, and was described as being intelligent, articulate and insightful. He came to therapy complaining of longterm impotence with women. He had recently become engaged to a charming widow, but after some months when the time came to set a date for the marriage, she decided that after all she did not wish to marry him.

Mr T. was a man who had longstanding difficulties of fear and guilt relating to his sexuality. He said of himself, 'My main difficulty is that I seem unable to form a fully loving relationship with a woman.'

He continued 'I have never married, although I have had a succession of friends, but none of the relationships have been particularly deep. I have always found women attractive and still do. I believe that it is still possible for me to find and love a woman in an intimate partnership. Despite my age I am still physically fit and young in heart. The impotence that I experience is, I am certain, due primarily to psychological and not physical factors. I am not homosexual, and have never had a homosexual relationship.'

Mr T. dated his sexual difficulties from his adolescence when he used to masturbate with fantasies of watching girls swimming and undressing. He was in the navy, but had no sexual contacts there. He had had a girlfriend 30 years ago, but she had had other affairs and he could not do anything with her; he was too shy even to be able to kiss her. He had another girlfriend whom his mother had criticized. At this time he was referred to a psychoanalyst, with whom he had worked on the problem for some years, but without anything really being achieved. During this time he had had intercourse once with a girl whom he knew to also be in analysis, and with whom he had been able to talk about his difficulties. After this one episode he had rejected her, and nothing more had come of the relationship.

Mr T. also told me the story of his father dying suddenly from a coronary when he was about 15, whereupon his mother had had a nervous breakdown for a year. Following this she suffered from long periods of depression, so he had had to care for her until she died when he was in his late 40s. Mr T. described his father as an alcoholic, but also a man who was very masculine. He said he spent time happily with him in the holidays until he died. I had no real picture of his father as having been much of a person in his life. His mother, however, was described as a depressive monster who destroyed anything of any real value to Mr T., as did his older brother, of whom he had always been afraid.

We considered Mr T. to be full of intellectual insight, but felt he was compliant rather than genuinely emotionally responsive. He gave the impression of being extremely emotional, crying a lot and demonstrating a good deal of inappropriate feeling.

Despite a poor prognosis for Mr T., I thought that it might in some ways be possible for us to try to help him work through part of his problem, particularly since his ex-fiancée was still about, and might, if he could change, be ready to try and help him overcome this particular block.

I tried hard to show Mr T. that his picture of how he might be an active, able and potent man was at odds with how an ordinary man might behave. His reply was to quote Shakespeare to me: 'The fault, dear Brutus, is not in our stars, But in ourselves, that we are underlings.'

I doubt if Mr T. believed that. He would tell me how marvellous I was, how much he envied what he took to be my success with women, and how he wanted to get my magic phallus inside him so that he too could be potent in the same way. My response was to point out that he was afraid to be ordinary and have an ordinary penis. His response was to tell me that I was a charming rogue, thus avoiding what endangered his feelings of safety. A sexual relationship with a responsive and loving woman was primarily a threat to him, and he did not want really to achieve what he had proclaimed he needed throughout his life

In fact, it turned out that he had been a transvestite as a youth, and had spent a great deal of time dressing up in his mother's clothes, filling condoms with water to simulate breasts, and masturbating before the mirror. There was an extremely perverse sexual relationship which underlay his problems, which I feel had never been properly treated. It seemed that he had tried to create a sado-masochistic homosexual relationship with me in which the secret satisfaction is to become the castrated but secretly powerful woman whom he both seeks and of whom he is terrified.

However, this is very far from being the whole story with older and ageing men. I will also mention the story of Mr R., who came to see me at the age of 75. He was a retired stockbroker, who had been widowed about two years before. He had a heart condition which necessitated a pacemaker, but otherwise was in good health. Mr R.'s problem was that, wishing to continue his sexual life following the death of his wife, he had advertised for a partner in the local newspaper. To his surprise, and subsequently to mine, he had received over 50 replies, suggesting that in his part of the world at least there was a large and unsatisfied population of sexually frustrated elderly women. Mr R. had worked his way methodically through the replies, and had finally settled on two of his respondents, one 25 and the other 15 years younger than he.

Mr R. had regular sexual relations with both women, and told me he was able to satisfy them both sexually. The problem that brought him to therapy was that while he could maintain his erection, he was no longer able to ejaculate and achieve sexual satisfaction. He could, however, masturbate to climax when alone.

I took Mr R. into therapy with me for a brief period. Rather than concentrating on his sexual difficulties, we worked on his mourning for his late wife, who turned out to have been a very formidable woman who had made many and varied demands on him during the period of her illness. Mr R. had given up his work when she fell terminally ill, and had nursed her devotedly during the five years that she survived.

This, coupled with some earlier traumata in his life, led me to suggest that he was in fact suffering from a guilt reaction. Indeed, it then appeared that Mr R. had been unable to give away his wife's clothes or in any way change her room since her death. Once we had begun to recognize the intense feelings of anger that he had had to suppress, particularly since he had had to live a celibate life for many years before her death, then his problems began to fall away. Mr R. gave her clothes to charity, reorganized his house, ended the relationship with the younger of his two ladies, who had turned out to be somewhat exploitative of him, and began to take the other lady away on trips to the Continent. Some months after the treatment finished he had to have his pacemaker replaced and had a slight upsurge in anxiety. I saw him for another few sessions, during which it became clear that he was now potent with his new female friend, who was kind and considerate. As she was free from marital ties, he intended to marry her in a few weeks' time.

In talking about sexuality as we age, I think that we have to recognize the possibilities for development and change as demonstrated by these people, and also the continued use of sexual longing and behaviour to help work through and cope with major life problems. It may end with a limited or self-destructive solution, such as the problem which haunted Mr T. through his life, where it was used in a perverse and fundamentally unsatisfying way to preserve a personal sense of safety, without any ongoing creative end. On the other hand, we also can recognize the creative aspects of sexuality, and we can promote these – in particular the capacity for intimacy.

3
Work

When Freud was asked for a definition of the basis of human happiness, he replied 'Liebe und Arbeit', which is usually translated as 'love and work'. It seems appropriate, then, to pass to the problems which arise in work roles as we age. There has been a very great change in work patterns in the West since the Second World War for a variety of reasons – partly cultural, partly economic and partly due to the erosion of family and local ties. Before the war it was customary for men to expect to enter a trade or a profession and remain there for life. Today, the man or woman who stays in one job for more than a few years is regarded as a failure, someone lacking in drive and ability. It is expected that people will move from job to job every few years as part of their career development, and even from country to country.

There is also enormous pace of technological change. This book is being written on a lap-top computer, which commands more power than the early machines which filled entire rooms. Fifteen years ago I would have dictated most of my written work to a secretary, who, having taken it down in shorthand, would have enjoyed the luxury of an electric typewriter on which to transcribe it. Computer experts tell me they already have produced prototypes which are able to transcribe dictation directly. It is likely that within the next decade there will be machines which will transcribe my voice directly on to the computer screen, whence it can be transmitted by fax, modem or optical fibre link to anyone with the appropriate technology to receive it.

Given this pace of change, it is not surprising that contemporary attitudes towards the ageing population are in a state of flux. On the whole, the young are more easily able to comprehend and use modern technology than those whose ways of thinking have been formed in a different era. My 12-year-old son sorts out problems with the computer without difficulty and almost instinctively; I have to laboriously read the manual and work through the examples before I can clear some trivial fault.

For many reasons there is a reinforcement of the notion that the ageing population represents a wasting asset, and that the modern capitalist economy will do well to divest itself of their help. Dealers in money markets tend to be clever young graduates who have the youthful capacity to keep up with the speed and intensity of global dealings, and expect to make a great deal of money before they burn out in their late 30s. The age of retirement for men in Great Britain has been falling rapidly, and recent statistics suggest that one-third of the male population over the age of 55 have in fact either been made redundant or have taken early retirement. This phenomenon is a new one which places great stress not only on those in middle age, but on the younger, and smaller, population who will have to support them in their later years.

In retirement we have in this century created a phenomenon which did not exist before. The really old were cared for, but until that time they and their families expected them to contribute to the general well-being by working as well as they could. In the 20th century, on the other hand, we have seen a long-term decline in the labour force, with a far greater likelihood that people will give up work in their middle to late 60s and fall – or be pushed – out of the labour market. This is due to the pace of technological change, but also to the delayed entry into the labour market of older women freed from the responsibility of child care and family. The unemployment rate of men between 55 and 65 is strikingly higher than that of women of the same age.

Another factor that is extremely important is the effect of differences in the type of work. Men with manual skills are far more likely to be forced into retirement than those with intellectual. Even among medical people there is an increased incidence of retirement among surgeons when compared to physicians, since the physical effort and co-ordination required of the surgeon shows a greater decrement in later life than the more intuitive skills of the physician.

Sad to say, once they have lost their employment, older people remain unemployed longer than younger ones. Personnel offices tend to be pessimistic about the capacity of older people to change and learn new ways of dealing with problems. In fact, the most recent studies show very clearly that older people can use accumulated experience to make up for deficits in learning speeds. Thus we have the paradoxical situation in which society offers support and money to those it considers to be too old to function in the employment market, while the actual beneficiaries feel they would be better off carrying out a job of any kind.

A typical example of the difficulty I am describing is Mr W. He is a good example of the difficulties that people find in remaining in the labour market after retirement:

Mr W. is now in his early 60s, having retired from the police force some years ago. He was an extremely physically powerful man who greatly enjoyed physical activities, and was extremely skilful with his hands. He had enjoyed his career in the police force, which had enabled him to harness his intense aggressivity into socially acceptable channels. A natural anarchist, Mr W. had always resisted promotion, which meant that he was able to use the service to support his lifestyle and have a most rewarding and enjoyable time.

Following the death of his wife from cancer, Mr W. was offered early retirement. This he gladly took, feeling that he could construct the sort of life that he wanted on the south coast, where he built himself a house and sailed regularly. For the first few years Mr W. was able to get whatever casual work that he needed to supplement his pension and to provide extra luxuries. However, the burden imposed by an unhappy and ill-judged second marriage – which he had entered into to reassure himself of his ongoing potency – meant that he found himself with considerable financial problems. As well, in a country in the depths of depression he was unable to find regular work. As Mr W. had recently been forced to have some orthopaedic surgery to correct an old injury, he was now also in receipt of a disability pension in addition to his occupational pension. This meant, however, that he was tied into a pension trap with no way of escape: he had just enough money without working to survive, but no work which would pay him enough to enable him to leave his second wife without selling his dearly loved house, most of which he had furnished with objects made with his own hands, but which was now greatly devalued in market terms. As one might well imagine, Mr W. was clinically depressed by all this, and felt hopeless and despairing.

I will contrast this with another man whom I also knew well, Mr L., who was for many years an extremely accomplished accountant. This was a profession for which Mr L. had trained at the behest of his parents, who were poor and ambitious for their clever son.

This, as Mr L. told me rather wryly, was well illustrated by the old saying 'Commit suicide or become an accountant'. A series of fortunate happenings when Mr L. was in his late 40s enabled him to give up work, which he did well but which he secretly loathed, and sell his partnership in his prosperous firm. For the first time in his life he was able to explore the possibilities of going to university. He decided to become a mature student, and graduated with honours and took up a new career in the arts with great success. Mr L. seems to be most happily settled into his new career and to be making good progress. His age and maturity, rather than being a hindrance are in fact a great help in that his judgement, and his excellent work habits provide him with the assurance and the stability for which younger men and women envy him greatly.

Work is for very many people a major form of antidepressant. The possibility of keeping up a valued working role even after retirement is of great importance. It seems that it will be necessary in our developing society to move from the sort of mentality that says a man may fly a 747 until the day before his 60th birthday, but ever afterwards he is absolutely forbidden to. We clearly need to provide a structure which will recognize the psychological needs of the person in late middle age and early old age, and help them through the transitional phase of gradually leaving the work force. Such institutions as the Universities of the Third Age are essential, and their remit should be widened and their possibilities made much clearer to all concerned.

Where people wish to work we shall need structures which permit them to do so. Equally, we shall need to recognize that the man or woman who says that now that he or she has retired they can spend all the time working on the garden is also a candidate for an early coronary or depressive illness when the idealized state yearned for in fact turns out to be far less ideal than imagined. It may well be that with the decline in birth rate and the economic burden on the labour force older people will once again be encouraged to work, and that the distinction between retirement and non-retirement will be blurred.

The capacity and the opportunity to go on working do not, however, necessarily lead to contentment and happiness. Let me describe W. about whom, when he was first referred to me at the age of 68, the referrer wrote:

'. . . his symptoms are a general sense of anxiety and insecurity manifested in fantasies about disasters happening to him and to people or animals who feel close to himself or to property such as his house. He constantly is plagued with the idea that illness, accidents and disasters are likely to happen. It seems that outside this narcissistic world, he has little feeling for people and can therefore deal quite coolly with emotional problems in others. He feels himself to be very withdrawn from life, relating only to his wife and to his work. The only relief from his anxiety occurs when he gets back to his flat in the evening and can drink a fair amount of alcohol. He uses drugs to sleep. He really cannot bear change.'

W. had had a very traumatic childhood. His mother seems to have been a very selfish and unmotherly woman who doted upon his homosexual elder brother. W.'s only close tie was to his nurse, who remained with the family until she died when he was 14. This nurse was clearly a woman who idealized W. and regarded him as if he were her own child. She was preoccupied with the idea that her charge would become ill.

W. was sent to boarding school at the age of eight, but lived only for the holidays when he could come home again. When he was 13 his parents separated. He felt guilty that he did not choose to stay with his father, but was terrified to tell his mother that he did not want to stay with her. Guilt towards his father seems to have been strong, as was the narcissistic loss at not having a father to identify with and idealize. He saw his father as having been progressively destroyed by his very powerful mother.

W. had a very timid and fearful adolescence, and then lived rather wildly as a young man. He was pleased that he had no children. His marriage had been stable, but before that he was riotous with women. He still feels guilty about this. We gradually came to understand that compulsive sexuality during his early years was a way of defending against his fears of abandonment – a fear of falling into nothingness or of falling apart. For him, continual sexual pursuit and the conquest of young attractive women, at whatever cost, were ways of keeping this fear at bay.

As he grew older and the pursuit of women became more problematic for him, W. turned to his work to give him the security which he needed. The firm for which he worked refused to hear of him retiring when he reached 70, and he continued full-time. Nevertheless, W. struggled against despair, ennui and sadness. His possessions were the only things which gave him pleasure. He lived in constant fear of being forced into retirement, which for him represented a terrifying loss. I became for him the voice of his sad, neglected and abandoned younger self – the vehicle for the feelings which he had had to defend against by a lifetime of denial – a denial in which desertion, the primal scene, and death all became identified as threats to his safety, and were defended against first by his promiscuity and then by his capacity to make deals for his firm.

His situation now is precarious in that his firm has been taken over and he has been told that at the end of his present contract he will be expected to retire at long last. Although W. and I have for many years tried to establish some activity that will bolster his self-image once the dreaded day arrives, he has always refused to contemplate the inevitable. Once work finishes he is sure that he will fall into a complete depression, and perhaps commit suicide.'

As we age, work becomes a major factor in our experience of being with others, as the basis of continued sense of personal continuity and meaning. Most older people move from an interactive world with others into a more internally focused world in which the debate is with the people who inhabit that inner world; the individual relates more to them than to the people outside.

As we age work then has a double purpose: it can become a major defence against the real or anticipated loss of the relationships which make life meaningful, or it can be used as a vehicle for adjusting to and developing the serenity which the individual may hope to achieve in the face of the gathering experience of the imminence and inevitability of death – both one's own death and that of those who are close and important to one.

4
Marriage

Until the second half of the 19th century, marriage in the West meant 'until death us do part'. From the standpoint of the late 20th century, this might mean 40 or 50 years. Yet we forget that for our forebears marriages on the average probably lasted little more than a decade, due to the ravages of disease and the high incidence of women who died in childbirth. Given that both spouses will live far longer than previously, and that marriage may well involve relationships lasting for many years, people have had to work out new patterns of marital existence. How can we imagine that a couple in their mid- to late 20s can possibly imagine what their lives will be like 10, 20 or 50 years later, and expect them to make provision – except of the most obvious sort – for what may or may not happen to them?

One solution developed since the Second World War has been the easy availability of divorce. Two hundred years ago, divorce was only open to the rich, while the poorer classes merely separated and moved on without benefit of clergy or anyone else. Today's no-fault divorces and the abolition of legal attribution of guilt and responsibility for the breakdown of marriages have gone some way towards meeting the situation which prosperity and longevity have created. It is estimated that at least half of today's marriages will end in divorce and potential remarriage for one or both partners. Indeed, the trend now seems to be away from formal marital status completely, with people raising families together but keeping their single status. There is also an increasing tendency towards the 'one-parent family' which will most probably lead towards greater anomie in society as the old family ties break down and dissolve, as they already seem to be doing in some parts of the United States.

The problems of the ageing couple who have stayed together are not easy to summarize. Part of the difficulty lies in the complexity of the motives that lead men and women to marry and create families in the first place. We know that people marry for a vast number of conscious and unconscious reasons. Psycho-dynamically, marriages symbolize and enact a whole series of layered unconscious phantasies for both parties, which may or may not be shared by the marital partners. The complexity and partial mutuality of the marital relationship mean it is fertile ground for both intimacy and antipathy throughout life.

As people age, the problems may become more evident and more painful. Once the parental imperative is either over or approaching its end, the couple will be left to face one another, and perhaps begin to work out problems and difficulties which they may have either consciously or unconsciously preferred to leave dormant during the parental years.

One of the most common patterns is that of the man in his mid-to-late forties who has nurtured a woman and their children for some 20 years or so. Such men often leave their wives for new, younger women, thus both maintaining their role as *pater familias* and managing to avoid confrontation with an older woman, who is now free to take on a more operative and aggressive role. On a deeper unconscious level such men are obviating the emergence in themselves of a more passive, feminine side which they fear and do not wish to experience. Interestingly, this is not a pattern that marriage counsellors and divorce specialists often see in reverse, as it seems to be relatively rare for women to leave their husbands for a younger man.

If marriage is fertile ground on which to work out neurotic conflicts, then the stresses of ageing can exacerbate the problems for the couple. The conscious or unconscious conflicts, or unconscious collusions, come under threat, and marriages may well start to unravel. Husband and wife begin to blame one another and try to seek a solution either within the marriage or outside, through friends or professional help. This may lead them into a settled, defensive system which can progress to the sort of fixed and invariant marital patterns which are well known in elderly couples. Or, it may permit them to review the marriage and its utility and lead to a search for new and more suitable partners with whom to build a system which will better meet their needs:

> Mrs B. was a 65-year-old woman referred to me because of the exacerbation of a fear of thunderstorms. For many years, whenever there was a storm she would have a panic attack and run out of the house. She and her now-retired husband, aged 70, had been married for 43 years. They had successfully brought up three children who had all left home.

With a female colleague I took this couple into marital therapy. It quickly became apparent that Mrs B.'s phobia reflected a lifelong fear of loss of control. This was reinforced by her very passive husband's reluctance to express any feelings to her or to engage in a row, even where it would have been appropriate and enjoyable to do so. Therapy with them led to their gradually becoming able to talk about some of the differences which had lain concealed for 43 years, and then to start to face some of the real dissatisfactions in their marriage. Sexual problems that could never be discussed before, which had their roots in childhood, were acknowledged for the first time.

Mrs B. was able to contemplate the fact that she and her husband might have to part unless some appropriate resolution of their problems could be found. Fortuitously, a thunderstorm occurred at this point in their therapy. When Mrs B. began to have her usual panic attack, her husband told her to shut up. Following the real row that ensued – perhaps the first row that they had ever had – he took her in his arms to comfort her: something that he would never have contemplated doing before. His own counterphobic needs, and having to deny his own fears of storms, which were the expression of a strongly repressed fear of both his own sexual drives and aggression had always intervened. He would later relate this to terrifying experiences of near drowning in early life, but at the time he was able to overcome this. They were able to make love in a satisfying and enjoyable way for the first time in many years.

While all this may sound somewhat banal, nevertheless this couple had a long history of undeclared suffering, which without therapeutic help might well have led them to finding solutions in psychosomatic illness or tranquillizers. These would have been something of a crutch, but would not have enabled them to be more open and loving with one another.

Among such patterns which are well known are the empty marriage. Here the couple live alongside one another in apparent harmony, but without any real exchange of information or feeling, each in their own groove and following their own interests but without any real meeting of the minds, and often bodies, at all. It is as if all that is left for these people is a kind of subclinical depression where they turn in on themselves and their own narcissistic states of mind and body. It seems to me that hypochondriasis and minor illness dominate the lives of such people, and that they are among the greatest consumers of tranquillizers and sedatives in the usual GP's list.

A second group, equally well known, are those who have elaborated a pattern of constant bickering. This group seem to keep themselves going through a well-rehearsed pattern of quarrels. These take up and repeat a number of themes which have gradually emerged from the infantile patterns which they are defending against at all times in their relationship, and which through the compulsion to repeat can be expressed and defended against in this way. Such marriages, although superficially more alive than the previous group, are in their own way as stereotyped and have little more potentiality for growth and change in old age. This group are less likely to change partners than the first, since their collusion is often extremely well worked out and, like Jack Sprat and his wife, they manage their joint neurosis well together.

A third group is represented by the marriage of convenience, where one or the other partner has married not out of love but for reasons such as a need to have children before it is too late, or to have a wife for the man's social position. Often such marriages also drift into a sort of slough of indifference, where the parties feel bound by obligation and not much more; there is no real affection or care for the other.

Ageing marriages have a very different feel to them than do those of younger people. One major reason for this, suggested by David Guttman[8], is that:

... late development and late onset pathology are often fuelled by the same forces. They are driven by the energies released in men and women in the course of the post-parental transition towards androgeny ... bisexuality does not become a significant problem, does not take on crisis proportions, until men and women stand down from the 'emergency' phase of parenthood. The gender distinctions get blurred as the last children are launched in the parent's middle years. Thus, when maturing children are demonstrating that they can assume major responsibility for supplying their own physical and emotional maturity, the stringent requirements of parenthood are relaxed and fathers and mothers can then reclaim the strivings and capacities that conflicted with the parental assignment and therefore had been either repressed or lived out vicariously through the spouse.

A great many of the interpersonal, unconsciously determined patterns which we can describe in marital relationships are linked to adulthood and its achievements. Assuming that we reach full adulthood with the birth of the first child rather than being given the key of the door at 21, then we have to describe a whole series of minor developmental stages which take place during the years before we pass into the Third Age at somewhere around 65 years or so.

Beginning with the birth of the first child, there is a period of intense dependency for the parent who is providing the major care for the infant. Winnicott speaks of a time of 'primary maternal preoccupation', during which the mother or the mothering person concentrates most of their mental and physical energy on the child. This of course involves a certain amount of neglect of family members, and some understanding on their part of the emotional needs that mothers have in this situation. Fathers may need to give up, for the time being, their own demands, which may well be rooted in their own early experiences, for satisfaction and being cared for and instead accept that there is a need for them to hold and contain in a relatively undemanding way the needs of the nursing couple. While such a role may be understood and enjoyed by some men who can recognize and identify with the love affair which is going on with the new member of the family, for others it represents an affront to them and their needs and can be the reason for very profound stresses in the marriage. This may even go so far in some cases as to lead to physical attacks on helpless infants because they are usurping the husband's place as the needy, dependent child.

Parents in the middle phase of a marriage have to re-negotiate role relationships – often on a fairly rigid basis. One of the problems of our contemporary society is that as work roles become more evenly spread between men and women, then the conflict as to who should stay at home and care for the needs of infants and children exacerbates conflicts within couples.

Today, many women have developed careers which they do not wish to abandon in their 30s in order to bear children. When they do decide that they should have families before the biological clock makes it too risky, they have no wish to give up more time than is necessary to the very difficult, time-consuming and demanding task of child rearing. The conflict between the needs of the partners, which was hitherto concealed by the pressure of social norms and expectations, can no longer be denied and can lead to intense and disruptive pressures within marriage. The stresses on adults from 25 to 45 are becoming more severe all the time. With the disappearance of the extended family and the support it could offer to couples in terms of child care and financial help, the possibilities of marital disruption are increasing exponentially. I have often come across couples at this stage where they express ruefully the wish that they both have that they could have an old-fashioned wife. Moreover, the existence of a large body of women who would be prepared to take on domestic tasks for others can no longer be counted upon, and the dependence of many families where both husband and wife work on using unskilled foreign teenagers as underpaid child minders and proxy parents has proved to be a recipe for disaster in many cases.

It should come as no surprise that when people enter the second half of life, defined rather arbitrarily by Elliott Jacques as commencing at the age of 37, one of the institutions which comes under the greatest strain is that of marriage. We all use our partners to represent and act out for us split-off, denied and idealized parts of ourselves and our former relationships with important people in the past. Where there has been a good match and people can accommodate reasonably to one another's needs, then the marriage can take the strain. However, if one or the other partner becomes particularly aware of some lack, this may lead to disruption of the relationship with unforeseen consequences.

While Jacques would have it that the passage at 37 is caused by the awareness in us that death may now be imaginable and indeed inevitable, we will certainly be aware of the changes that time has wrought in our sexual performance, our appearance, our capacity to remember and create, and in our relationships with others. In a particularly youth-oriented society such as ours, this is bound to have repercussions – and the marriage will have to deal with the impact of ageing.

There has not been a great deal of interest in psychoanalytic thinking concerning the problems of marriage. Certainly, there has been very little published on the problems of the ageing couple. Yet as people age they have to face the continuing and often cumulative stress of living with another person who may have developed personally in a totally unexpected direction over the years. It is a commonplace of psychoanalytic theory that this will entail the reworking of earlier developmental conflicts in the context of contemporary stresses. However, how this is to be done is not often spelled out, and workers in the field are left to struggle with these problems without much in the way of guidance or support.

One area in which there may be conflict is that of dependence versus independence. It is often galling for the older man to find that after retirement, or perhaps some developmental deficit such as a mild stroke or another physical illness, that he has become far more dependent on his wife than he would have expected. Such mundane questions as who is going to drive the car can become foci of anger and anxiety in quite marked ways. One elderly woman, whose husband in his youth had participated in the Targa Florio and the Mille Miglia, found herself in considerable difficulties when he refused to stop driving in his late 70s. He insisted that his skills had in no way diminished, and even the fact that, due to his unacknowledged cerebral insufficiency, he had been unable to recognize the road where their daughter lived had not been sufficient either for him to accept what had happened or to recognize his own difficulties. Having been a very obsessional man whose identity was very much bound up with his achievements both in his own professional field and in his driving, to have to rely on his wife in this area of his life would have been literally insupportable. The result was that their capacity to move about was almost completely destroyed.

Another pathological pattern that has been described by workers in this field the oppositional couple. In this pattern,

> . . . oppositional argument replaces the direct expression of feelings, particularly those pertaining to dependency needs and the suffering resulting from experiences of rejection, criticism and disapproval. The oppositional style of argument is used by the couple as a joint defence against revealing dependent longings and feelings of being inadequate and unloveable.[9]

The author says that one can distinguish such fighting from ordinary marital spats, and that there are two types of oppositional fighting, each linked to a different early developmental level. The first of these is the symbiotic dependent type, where the couple become and remain involved in a resentful, clinging, hostile, clutching type of relationship. In these couples, as they age the resentment that has been there from the beginning – since each needs the other to be the desired mother of early infancy, and each has naturally to fail to reach the desired standard – mounts cumulatively and then becomes established as the medium of exchange between the couple. As they age, unless there are some reasons for changing this pattern, it becomes more and more firmly established with the result that they become mired in a miasma of discontent and pain.

There is not a great deal that one can do to help such unhappy people since almost by definition what they desire – whether it takes the form of sexual satisfaction, attention, closeness and warmth – can never be achieved without destroying the internal idealized picture which they have established to make up for their early losses. Even if their partner were to become the understanding person for whom they claim to be searching in one or other of these spheres, they merely transfer their demands and their complaints to another area of their joint lives. As people age, their demands inevitably become even less easy of satisfaction so that the grumbling and lack of pleasure almost become a way of life for them. Their children and their friends tend to regard them with a jaundiced eye, and they gradually alienate those close to them, remaining locked in a painful and unhappy relationship rather than being able to develop new and appropriate interests to deal with the onset of ageing.

The second, higher-level type of interaction has to do more with the shared internalization of a very critical, demanding, authoritarian parent or parents who have markedly influenced the life of each spouse through their demands. By projection, each member of the couple perceives his or her partner as the controlling and manipulative parent of their childhood and finds themselves in the position of needing to constantly battle to refrain from being overwhelmed and destroyed by the other. Naturally, because of the need to be loved and protected, any victory over the partner and over the internal object has to be entirely temporary. If the victory is complete then the person will run the risk of losing the good aspects of the internalized objects, particularly their capacity to provide a safe and reliable framework for the individual. With these couples one finds oneself in the position of being a referee, with the added handicap that although they may ask you for help in trying to resolve their problems, they may equally well gang up against you, having made you into the repository of their bad objects. These patients are far easier to help, and they often have a better work record and interaction which they can use to provide backup as they age. The difficulty lies more in the normal rigidities of thinking, about which I talk at greater length in another chapter of the book.

Most of the research that has been published in recent years seems to suggest that there is a gradually or steeply decreasing curve of marital satisfaction. This starts with a high level at the time of the honeymoon, a major dip when children arrive with their needs and demands, and then either a slow decrease or a plateau which seems to denote a generalized indifference. It seems to be true, however, that there are some marriages where the couple find that the increased freedom that comes with material success and the coincidental departure of the children releases them to work out their own personal satisfactions in hitherto unexpected ways. Sometimes we see the possibility of a shared experience in later life which impresses the bystander by its richness and variety. However, the general pattern seems much as I have described it above.

Kuypers and Bengtson[10] suggest that members of an older family – one with adult children – have profoundly conflictual loyalties. This conflict is particularly severe for the middle generation, the ageing parents. They define the following steps in their argument.

First, as families age, the intensity of family involvement will decrease. It is clear that the family is a base from which the children will eventually depart. Insofar as parents expect to make sacrifices for the sake of infants and children, they can look forward to a stage when their children's needs no longer need be regarded as paramount. With the end of adolescence the parents will be freer to live their own lives and not have to put their children's needs before their own. There is little expectation of the original situation remaining static.

Second, as families age, primary loyalties will transfer. As the children grow up and leave home, so their attachment to their family of origin will decrease. They will expect to found new families, and in that way distance themselves from their parents and their siblings. This presents real problems for their parents, who may in no way wish to sever the ties which bind them to their children in the same way in which the children wish to be free. The whole problem of ambivalent feelings towards children and what they have taken from one then arises. Ageing parents may well have very strong feelings of animosity and resentment towards their children, who have a freedom and opportunities which they sacrificed for their sake and can have careers and relationships which for one reason or another were not available to their parents.

Third, parents care for their children and not the reverse. On the whole, most parents continue to feel that their role as parents will continue throughout the life-cycle, and the children also feel that it is difficult to give up the dependent role to which they have always been accustomed.

It might be expected that these expectations would only gradually be eroded, and that the nuclear family would change in a harmonious way as the parents age. However, whether one takes a family systems point of view or a psychoanalytic one, it is seldom that matters proceed so smoothly. In the first place, there is very often a great deal of conflict between children and parents as the children forge their own identity. It is hard, particularly in our youth-centred culture, for the parents who may have striven hard for financial security to see a youth in his mid-20s who can earn close to a six-figure salary. This sets up an immediate conflict and revives all the Oedipal problems concerning potency and aggression in both father and son. The problem faced by the ageing parent is indeed an acute one, and not something that can be easily negotiated by either side. It means that the father has to tread warily and cannot as in the past expect that his son will look to him as a source of guidance and superior experience, as he probably did to his own father. All the expectations of taking a mentor role have to be abandoned, and this may well arouse a great deal of conflict in the family.

Equally, the revolution in sexual relationships and behaviours which we have experienced since the Second World War are inevitably reflected in the relationships between parents and children. Children nowadays regard sexual experience, both hetero- and homosexual, in a completely different light than did their parents' generation. The ageing adults faced with abortion on demand, the sexual freedom of the young, politically conscious thinking, and the AIDS epidemic are almost certain to find their

most profoundly held beliefs challenged and often contemp-
tuously dismissed. Mothers find that their daughters no longer
think in terms of conventional marriage, but live with 'partners'
and have children with them, or even find the notion of being a
single-parent family in no way strange.

The conflict between the values of the parents as internalized in
their ego-ideals and experiences of their own families of origin is
often a painful and distressing one, and one that leads to various
forms of neurotic and psychosomatic illness in parents as they age
and have to come to terms with the differing morals and
behaviours of their children. Instead of living in a well-ordered
world where their achievements and their opinions can be held in
respect, they only too often find themselves on the sidelines,
feeling ignored and even dismissed as not having anything of value
to add to the questions which their children are seen to be
addressing.

For the parents it is often extremely difficult to identify the
areas of dissonance between them and their children in a way
which can be addressed and worked with in the family. We have
all seen the bewilderment which older people express as their
dearly loved children develop in ways which they find distressing
and unacceptable.

For the child-now-become-adult, it is perhaps easier to deal
with the problem by splitting their image of the parent or parents
into two or more parts. The parent is then both guarded as the
cherished and respected figure of childhood and infancy, and
treated as such at moments such as birthdays or Christmas, while
denigrating and rejecting the often cherished and lifelong belief
systems of the parent, thus denying them their hard-won
experience and the rewards that come from observing an ethical
code over part or all of a lifetime.

This experience of denial is particularly hard for the ageing
person to accept, even more when the child emphasizes the effect
of the person's ageing on their judgement and understanding of
important issues which they both share concern about.

Some authors have suggested that the typical response from
parents under these circumstances is to avoid action and deny that
any crisis – whether located in the child or in the circumstances of
the parents – necessitates action. When faced by such challenges,
the easiest thing for the ageing parent is to retreat into denial and
do nothing. One patient told me that when he told his father that

at the age of 27 he intended to marry, his father replied, 'I don't like the sound of that – I'm too young to become a grandfather.'

Equally, of course, such family crises may happen the other way round. The ageing parent who has at long last freed himself or herself from the ties and demands of dependent children, may suddenly find that the grandparents, his own parents, who had managed until this time to live in reasonable independence and not make too much demand on the ageing individual for provision, may now need both physical and psychological care at just the moment when they consider themselves entitled to a new and creative freedom. This brings into play all kinds of conflicts concerning what is due to the individual and how to deal with the new dependency. I suspect that many of the stress symptomatologies which one encounters during this time of people's lives has far less to do with the menopause and physiological change and far more to do with the demands that such problems place upon the individual.

The type of marriage which is based upon collusion, which is shallow and not rooted in real understanding and intimacy, will not provide the psychological support that is needed under these circumstances. It must be almost impossible for the idealized and spoilt man or woman who has been infantilized by their partner, as part of a need to preserve a good internal object, to emerge from this role and be a real support when their partner is faced with an elderly parent who may be dying.

Partners in a marriage bring with them all kinds of baggage which is linked to their own early struggles for autonomy and authenticity. Ageing brings with it intense problems to do with both parental and child figures. There seems no doubt that these can be supported or made worse by one's marital partner. The unconscious expectations in the face of the stresses of both dependence and independence highlight what is there and not there in the marriage. It is hard for a man or woman who is fighting out inside themselves what is appropriate or inappropriate in their response to their parents' decline to find themselves targeted by their partners at one and the same time. In some ways the middle years of a marriage represent a time of great vulnerability when sympathy and loving kindness are at a premium, yet when the circumstances of the relationship make it more than hard to mobilize what is necessary.

As an illustration of what I mean, I would like to talk about Ina, who was a woman in her early 50s who had made a late marriage to a rather narcissistic and self-centred man whom I shall call John.

John had been married before and had been divorced by his first wife. He had two daughters and a son by his first wife, on whom he had made an over-generous settlement. His children disliked Ina, but she did her best to keep on good terms with them and even invited them to live with them when they were at university. The marriage was based on her need for a very masculine and potent father to replace the father with whom she had had a close, intimate but not sexual relationship in her childhood. Her mother had been degraded by them both, and was indeed a woman from a rather less socially prominent background than her father.

All went reasonably well until John began to be attracted to the wife of a colleague who lived in an open marriage, and for her own reasons encouraged his advances. This woman was even younger than Ina, and satisfied better John's need to be the fatherly male as well as his sexual phantasies. This relationship gradually became an affair and Ina had to struggle with her conflict between her need to keep her husband and her fury that his narcissistic needs were so belittling to her. They kept things going on a very precarious basis: he was unwilling to give up his paramour, and she was unwilling to give him up, as she had been unwilling to give up her narcissistic father.

Things came to a head when Ina's mother developed a carcinoma, which meant that Ina and her siblings felt that they should do their best to spend time with her. Ina was devastated when she discovered that John refused to come with her to share her agony and her depressive guilt about her mother and her needs. He was in fact spending the weekends when she went down to see her mother with his lover.

Ina was faced with a conflict between duty and her rage with her husband, who was refusing to accept her need for him to support her. Her compromise was to refuse to recognize the very clear signs that her mother was on the point of death, and instead to insist on spending a weekend with John. After her mother's death she had a depressive breakdown, which was answered by John's developing coronary heart disease, from which he died a year later. Ina feels angry, empty and cheated in every way by life and that there is very little that is worth going on for.

A similar pattern can be seen in Saul. The third child and only son in a very unhappy middle class family, he had been his mother's pride and joy. In his early childhood, he had climbed into bed with her at every opportunity, and while she had not actually physically seduced him, he got a great deal of what he recognized as physical pleasure in rubbing himself up against her body. This love affair had been violently interrupted by his father, who had physically ejected him from the marital bed and forbidden him to return. Saul had been profoundly narcissistically wounded by this, and throughout his childhood had always sided with his mother against his father. As he reached adulthood, Saul rebelled against his father's ways of thinking, and always treated him as if he were not someone of whose views he needed to take any cognizance.

Saul had great difficulty in finding a wife who would meet his exacting standards. When he finally did marry it was to a woman who was superficially very perfect but who was in fact something of a slob underneath. He spent a great deal of his time bemoaning this fact, but was gradually able to understand that he was in this way being the mouthpiece of his mother and her rejection of her own messy femininity.

Saul's world was turned upside down when his mother came down with a serious illness and was devotedly nursed by her despised husband, who in his turn fell ill. His mother would do nothing about it and left her husband to himself, so that his bed was never made and he was very badly cared for. Saul, who had distanced himself to another town, eventually was so over-come after a visit that he asked the family doctor to intervene.

Within days Saul's father had had to be hospitalized, and he died shortly thereafter of kidney failure. Saul was able to be with him and recognize how much he needed and wished for a worthwhile relationship with a loving man, and he and his father were able to make a good farewell to one another before the father died. Saul was enormously grateful for this experience, which led him on to examine his other relation-ships to see if they too should be rethought. He found that there was a great deal of unexpressed fury with his mother, and was able to see that this was mirrored by his relationship with his wife. In working this out with me it became possible for Saul not to be so perfectionistic in his demands on her and their children, so that the marriage has become a source of positive support for him as he tries to deal with his mother's ageing and prospective death.

5
Thinking

Sigmund Freud said in 1905, 'Near or about the 50s, the elasticity of the mental process, on which the treatment depends, is as a rule lacking – old people are no longer educable.'[11] This is patently a false statement, which is based on a sexual analogy, and in no way fits either Freud himself, who was to completely recast his whole theory some 12 years later, in his 60s(!), nor the world in which he lived, where there were many creative, active and subtle intelligences belonging to people in their late 50s and 60s who were constantly producing new work.

There is now abundant evidence that it is possible to treat people psychotherapeutically in later life successfully, and that such people can change and grow in a thoughtful and creative manner. It seems likely that Freud was giving voice to an idea which is rooted in folklore, namely that ageing and mental deterioration are synonymous. The Carnegie Report[12] identified areas where education, training and information can contribute to well-being in the Third Age. Thus,

> . . . for the individual the Third Age is a time of emerging from the imperatives of earning a living and bringing up children and personal development can once again become a central concern. Individuals will, however need to rely more on themselves to seek out a range of activities and build a network of links with different people . . . Education, training and information have an important role in enriching the lives of Third Agers, and giving them the knowledge, confidence and skills to develop a range of activities of their choice.

It is a very sobering thought that two-thirds of those now between 50 and state retirement age left school by 15 years old. Many of those who now are free to pursue further studies would wish to do so – roughly one in four of those aged 55 to 64 and 15 per cent of those aged 65 and over. The Carnegie Report shows that older people can learn as well as younger ones provided learning is self-pacing and practical rather than by memorizing instructions, and preferably builds on earlier experience.

Nevertheless, according to the Report there are a wide range of barriers which exist and which tend to depress people's aspirations and participation: attitudes of the clientele, employers, providers and society at large; timing, location and the physical environment of classes; lack of information and guidance; money. That said, many of the Third Agers, particularly those who left school early, think education is not for them, and are surprised at the scope, relevance and welcoming nature of education if they do try it. They also often find that they gain more than they expected in terms of confidence and the ability to develop new friendships and activities.

One of the most frequent examples we meet of the relationship between ageing and cognition is when we forget the names and titles of people whom we earlier recognized and could give names to without difficulty. Some of us find this easy and often funny – for others it is like the cloud which presages senile dementia in just a few years' time. Charles de Gaulle asked his secretary to tell him if he seemed to be losing his memory, since that would be the sign which would lead him into immediate retirement and the abandonment of office. Not all politicians are as scrupulous as this – Winston Churchill continued as prime minister after having had a serious stroke, which was concealed from Press and public by his doctors. Nevertheless, for most of us the early signs of cognitive deficit are regarded as ominous and frightening.

The question of intellectual abilities and how to maintain them as we age has been studied fairly fully in recent years. The picture which now seems to be emerging is quietly reassuring. Psychologists used to say that intelligence peaked at age 16 and that it was all downhill thereafter. More recently the age of intellectual primacy has been brought forward to 35 with no great decline until the early 60s, where one's intelligence was comparable to the level which it reached in the 20s.[13] This makes much better sense than the earlier estimates, which went against common experience:

> On the nature of the creative process at its peak and the nature of its decline, we are still very dependent on the auto-biographical notes of very gifted people. [He quotes Mary Cartwright, a mathematician, as saying] 'No mathematician should ever allow himself to forget that mathematics, more than any other art or science, is a young man's game . . .

Newton gave up mathematics at 50 and he had lost his enthusiasm long before . . . I believe that major advances [in this field] are usually obtained by approaching a subject from a slightly different angle from that usually adopted, ideas often coming in the course of approaching, that is learning, the subject. When it is fully understood, interest often wanes and ideas become fixed . . . But I have only shifted the subject in saying that older people find it less easy to learn. Speaking for myself, I feel that my brain is less persistently active than it used to be, and I feel that declining mental energy is the real answer.'

The author goes on to consider the changes in strategies that are deemed to be necessary by older people in order to cope with this perceived decline in mental energy. He says that contrary to the evidence which has been available from studies of short-term intelligence, such as test results, we have to consider the ways in which older individuals define and try best to achieve their long-term goals. He was surprised to find that in fact the older individuals were used to changing and redefining these goals on a more frequent basis then younger people. As a result, far from being considered rigid in their thinking they were in fact rather more flexible than younger men and women. Moreover, they showed a recognition of the necessity for a greater discipline and for better control of affect towards colleagues and juniors, and this tolerance was recognized in their definition of their goals.

One of my patients, a businessman who retired at the age of 83, was an excellent example of this type of intelligence. He had been in this particular sphere for more than 50 years, and there was nothing new which anyone could teach him about the problems which he encountered daily. However, in his deal-making he was far more flexible than his younger colleagues, and he coupled this with a most scrupulous commitment to any deal which he had made, even if it turned out to be to his own disadvantage. As a result he was trusted by his rivals as well as his customers, and he remained successful until he was forced unwillingly to retire because of a change in long-term corporate strategy.

Other coping strategies include the fact that the elderly are much more aware of the need for taking advice, and indeed do so far more readily than younger people. They are aware of the need to conserve time and resources of energy, and judge better the distinctions between critical tasks and those which could be put on one side or left to others to carry out.

Despite this, in many ways Alzheimer's Disease and the other forms of cognitive deficit have become symbols for our age of a dreaded and unmentionable fate, with their picture of senile dementia, helplessness and uselessness. Modern medicine keeps many alive who in former times would have succumbed to various forms of illness. The downside of this is the fear of surviving to a time when there is nothing left to live for, and no help or understanding of one's existential situation. It might well be said that we are not that far away from Dean Swift's Struldbrugs on the Isle of Laputa – beings who had been given the gift of immortality and were now helplessly senile.

The problem of senescence and ageing is one which nowadays, like death, seems to be swept under the carpet. Recent years have seen a great efflorescence of old people's homes, where the old can be deposited by their families and cared for by others. The most recent statistics suggested that no less than five per cent of our aged populations are in this type of care, which is not based on a long-term professional training, nor has the standards of quality control which one would wish.

A few years ago two of my students and I were asked if we could help with a programme of care for just this population at an NHS hospital which had both a geriatric and a psychogeriatric service. The ward to which we were invited to consult consisted of a part of an old workhouse which had been very badly adapted to the needs of a geriatric population. It consisted of a large room into which some 20 old women had been crammed. They each had a bed and an exiguous locker for their few possessions. During the day the staff got them out of bed and parked them in front of a television set, which was constantly on. They were offered physiotherapy and some forms of occupational therapy of a not-very-demanding kind.

When we first came to the ward, we found that the nursing staff were very resistant to anything that we might offer them. The matron had damned us with faint praise, and the consultant had told them that we came from a psychoanalytic institution and that we would help them. Within weeks he announced that he shortly would be leaving to take up a job in another hospital. We felt that there was very little that we could do directly to reach the patients, but we offered an experiential group to those on the nursing and ancillary staffs who wished to join. To our surprise, some eight people joined us, and we were able to work with them for the next year.

We found that there was a great deal of care for these very deteriorated patients among the staff, and that they could identify with them and their needs to quite a marked degree. Many of the old ladies had no family who ever came to visit them, and they looked after their pensions and their few belongings in the most scrupulously careful way.

In the group it became clear that the staff wished to do far more for the patients than was allowed by the hospital, and would willingly have tried to stimulate them by taking them on outings and making their lives more interesting. They were hampered by the rules of the nursing hierarchy, and by the need to treat the patients as if they were objects to be fed and kept clean; the lack of sufficient numbers meant that they could do very little to stimulate them while at the same time needing to attend to their basic needs. Parking them for the day in front of the television screen, while it was frustrating, was about all that there was time for them to do. Nevertheless, the staff did seem to be able to make contact with the women.

One of their major complaints was that when a patient died they were not permitted to leave the bed empty for a few days in order to focus their mourning, but instead had to replace her with another patient immediately because of the fiscal needs of the new-look health service.

I am glad to say that we were able to facilitate the expression of the nurses' feelings in such a way that they were able to go to their senior nursing officers and explain their difficulties. The result was that when the ward was transferred to new premises later in the year, they were consulted about the physical setup and their suggestions were listened to. Greater amounts of space were made available, and much more varied forms of care were provided in the new and more salubrious premises. I would have liked to carry out a proper research study on this ward comparing both the patients' needs for medications with that on a ward where the staff did not have the same opportunity to ventilate their feelings, and to consider the proportion of staff absenteeism from stress syndromes and physical ailments.

There is nothing particularly startling in this type of

intervention. What it does suggest is that it is possible to make an end to the 'warehousing' of old people, and treat them with dignity even if they are in the last stages of senile dementia. For those whose plight is not so great, there is a great deal more that can be done.

One approach which seems to have a great deal to offer is that put forward by Cohler, who draws on self-psychology as developed by Kohut to establish his argument that there is an epistemic drive which is as vital as the sexual and aggressive drives in establishing identity throughout the life course. [14] In Cohler's view, we are all involved in revising our view of our own lives as we continue the life course. Helping people to look at their lives as they progress, and thus revise their views of what has happened to them and its meaning for themselves and others is a most effective therapy. This leads to greater reconciliation with the failures as well as the successes of the past. Research workers in this field have called this experience the 'legitimization of biograpy' justifying to oneself decisions and actions over the course of a lifetime.

Cohler goes on to suggest that if people can believe that their time was well spent in the past, then they can hope that the remaining time will be put to good use. This leads to the conviction that a sense of personal coherence and integration can be maintained despite the recognition of the nearness of death. Indeed, one of the key points that Cohler makes is that as we age there is a major difference between being alone and being lonely. He says,

> As family and friends die, move or become incapacitated, there may be diminished access to forms of support that was taken for granted earlier in life. At the same time, with the increased use of reminiscence, first in middle age as a means to solve problems and later in life to provide comfort and preserve a sense of meaning and a continuity of experience, being alone is less disturbing and even desirable, since it allows time for reflection. Despite being foreshortened, the present becomes meaningful through its connection to the past. This connection provides a sense of personal integration. Families and friends may move away or die; memories do not.

Interestingly, Cohler suggests that at least part of the terror inspired by cognitive impairment such as Alzheimer's is the loss of memory and the ability to reminisce, and thus, ultimately, a breakdown in personal integration.

6
Striking the Balance

The ageing process is a complex and difficult one for most of us. Among the complaints which are most frequently expressed are unhappiness, alienation, the loss of self-esteem, desolation and insecurity. This is a fairly formidable list, yet one with which those who work with ageing people will easily recognize. I think this is the reason why so much of the literature on the ageing process is linked to loss, as in many of the examples which I have cited earlier in this book. There is an expectation that ageing is a process of deterioration, and that there is nothing which can be done to either halt or ameliorate the process. As I have suggested, this is only part of what is involved. Nevertheless, it is hard to talk nowadays about the rewards of ageing since we have a perspective which thinks in terms of youthfulness as being the prime of life.

From a psychoanalytic point of view, it is only to be expected that individuals should feel unhappy as they age. After all, we lay down expectations in our infancy and childhood about the sort of people we would like to become when we are ourselves adults. Many of us daydream of winning the 1500 metres' race in the Olympic Games, or being another Zuleika Dobson, with all the young bloods of Oxford throwing themselves into the Isis for love of our wit and beauty. These daydreams are rationalizations of the feelings of inferiority and dependence which we are bound to have in relation to our parents, no matter how kind, understanding and supportive they may have been. They often act as the drivers towards many kinds of distinction, and may well be very effective as ways of supporting us as we struggle to find a métier in life.

Such idealizations are also at the root of our search for partners and lovers. As even a cursory reading of the psychoanalytic literature will demonstrate, there are always very marked unconscious meanings underlying all our aspirations. Inevitably, therefore, both our own achievements and the personality and behaviours of those close to us are liable to lead to disappointment and pain.

One of the commonest syndromes which we encounter is one I call 'the failed Nobel Prize winner'. The fact that someone has shown themselves to be talented has led either the individual or those close to him or her to expect that they will succeed and have some modicum of success in the field which they have chosen. Naturally, a few do succeed, either because they are genuinely talented or through good fortune. The great majority of us do not succeed to a point which fulfils our fantasies. We may well have worked our way up the ladder and the prize looks well within our grasp, when it is snatched away:

Mr P. worked for many years in a large and prestigious institution, grinding out the various appointments which he had been allotted. It was confidently anticipated that he would become the group managing director in three years' time, when the present incumbent retired. Sadly for him the firm succumbed to a takeover bid, and instead of reaching the goal for which Mr P. had sacrificed a large part of his life and a considerable degree of his family's happiness, he was abruptly dismissed and another executive from an outside firm who was in favour with the new owners was brought in to take his place. Mr P. was desperately disappointed and unhappy about this, since his disturbed and unhappy childhood with a very cold and remote father had led him to try and reach this glittering prize and in that way try and satisfy and give pleasure to his very forbidding internal objects. It was as if some internal prediction that he would never be good enough to live up to his father's expectations of him had really come true. He was offered and took a teaching job in a nearby university, but for Mr P. teaching business methods in no way compensated for the power and prestige which in his view, he had quite unfairly lost.

This theme of loss of self-esteem is one which resonates through working with ageing people, and is something which the therapist or analyst has to constantly be on his or her guard against in order to deal with properly. It is particularly evident in all walks of life where the nature of training and skills are changing all the time. Mr P. was a businessman of the highest calibre, a graduate of Oxbridge who had given up the possibility of a career in the creative field to achieve the security and power which his internal objects demanded of him. He was at least able to find a substitute activity in a neighbouring field. For the blue-collar worker the same kind of opportunity often simply does not seem to exist. Men and women who are made redundant because their skills can be replaced by a machine or whose work can be more cheaply carried out by lower paid labour in Third World countries often find themselves on the scrapheap. If they are in the second half of life, they will have little or no hope of finding an acceptable job in the foreseeable future.

It is a criticism of our society that no real thought has been given to the support and rehabilitation of such people. While the psychotherapist can do something to alleviate the personal pain and unhappiness of individuals, far too much is left to social services, the GP with his tranquillizers and anti-depressants, and the efforts of the individuals and their families themselves.

Latest figures suggest that the UK has a core unemployed population of one and a half million people, and there is very little in the way of provision for their needs. This situation can only worsen in the next few years, since I see from my computer magazines that the technology has now been perfected for the first hand-held 'notepad' that will transform handwriting into type, and I understand that voice recognition is already possible for computers with the result that as technology comes down in price with demand there will be a marked decrease in the need for secretarial staff in offices and elsewhere. There seem to be no plans or provision for the economical and psychological needs of the vast numbers of people who will be displaced by this latest development in the communications revolution.

After the Second World War, attachment theory, as put forward by John Bowlby, provided the rationalization which took many women out of the labour market and forced them to stay at home to look after small children, who were conveniently hypothesized to be at risk if they were separated from their mothers for even a very short space of time. I do not wish to minimize the importance of Bowlby's work, but it took the return of the warriors to bring his theories into public acceptance. It will be interesting to see what sort of theory will emerge to deal with this coming critical period, and its consequences.

Many people deal with the problem through withdrawal and isolation. Kingsley Amis has delineated much of the psychology and psychopathology of this group in his novel *The Old Devils*, which portrays the way in which a group of elderly middle-class Welshmen and women cope with problems of isolation and loneliness, which retirement and the feeling of being on the shelf brings with it. There is copious resort to alcohol to deaden the pain and to try and provide some narcissistic satisfaction. Alcoholism is a major problem in the ageing population, but for many it does provide a cushion to help them through what may well turn out to be a series of formless and uninteresting days.

The tendency to withdraw and develop paranoid ideation is one which is only too prevalent, and one antidote is the formation of groups which at worst can provide some sort of external support for the individual and enable them to locate persecutors outside the boundaries of the group, thus providing some safety and shared experience. On a more positive level, older people can be encouraged to join vocational and interest groups, and to interest themselves in many types of activity. It seems terribly sad that so little provision is made, however, and that one of the few activities that are available to alert and intelligent elders is attendance at such free public spectacles as the Law Courts.

Companionship becomes more and more essential for people who have little left in the way of vocational interest, and even the slightest of everyday activities can assume a very great importance. Recent research has highlighted the importance of pets, with their response to tactile communication, for old people's survival. The spinster and her cat is a proverbial theme in literature.

One real investment that the community could make would be the provision of various self-help groups for the ageing population. As we will see later, there seems evidence that although the raw speed and effectiveness of thinking naturally declines with age, this is amply compensated for in the ageing individual by the capacity to scan the field and arrive at solutions by using a process of lateral thinking. This tends to evolve in response to the gradual and often imperceptible losses in the ageing process.

One well-known example concerns that brilliant tactical thinker, the first Duke of Wellington. When the Great Exhibition of 1851 was first opened in 1851, the vast Crystal Palace was plagued with a completely unforeseen infestation by the common London sparrow, which threatened to lay a thin layer of mess and untidiness over the whole sparkling edifice and its contents. Those responsible for the Exhibition were driven close to despair, with the result that Queen Victoria decided to consult the Duke, who was then in his 80s and regarded by her as the repository of all wisdom. On this occasion, his tactical genius gave her the immediate and sensible answer that Prince Albert and the scientists and engineers had not been able to discern. 'Sparrowhawks, Ma'am, sparrowhawks' was the immediate answer. The Duke had seen through to the heart of the problem and found the answer, which had escaped the scientists.

This is one of the great changes which have taken place in this century; the whole notion of the wisdom of the elders and their capacity to make a worthwhile contribution has been abandoned. It may be that this is due to the pace of technological change or the enormous physical stresses that power in our society places upon individuals. Any account of the workload carried by the ordinary government minister suggests that such a workload would tend to break any but an extremely fit and healthy man or woman. There seems however, a recurring need for someone who can stand back from the fray, above the battle as it were, and bring a sense of balance and authority to matters. Such advisers are woefully few, and their absence perhaps goes some way towards explaining the sense of expediency and playing for short-term advantage which seems to permeate the activities of our politicians on a day-to-day level.

The possibility of fulfilling such a role is of course much greater in artistic than business fields. For creative artists seem to work on a very different time scale than do those in executive positions. While a manager can lose his effectiveness and usefulness by the time that he reaches his 60th birthday, the artist may still be in the process of intensive exploration of his internal and external worlds. Elliot Jacques, in his seminal paper on the mid-life crisis[15] makes an interesting distinction between the work of creative artists in their 20s and early 30s, where creativity seems to spring from some inner fire, and the later work of such people, where there is a much more sculpted and considered quality to what they do.

It is essential that later life should not be regarded as a period of deficit. In many ways, later life in our society is a time of fulfilment and content for many people. Education, training and information can have an important role in enriching the lives of Third Agers and giving them the knowledge, confidence and skills to develop a range of activities of their choice.

It will be clear that we have to make greater provision for older people so that they do not feel that they have been placed on the scrap heap after retirement and instead can find ways of using their skills and knowledge. The psychoanalytic writer who has contributed most to this area of research and understanding has undoubtedly been George Pollock, one of the outstanding workers in this field over many years. Pollock has suggested in a series of papers that later life offers the opportunity for individuals to focus on and work through what he has called 'the mourning-liberation process':

> The basic insight is that parts of the self that once were, or that one hoped might be, are no longer possible. With the working out of the mourning for a changed self, lost others, unfulfilled hopes and aspirations, as well as feelings about other reality losses, there is an increasing ability to face reality as it is and as it can be. 'Liberation' from the past and the unattainable occurs. New sublimations, interests and activities appear. There can be new relationships with old 'internal objects' as well as new objects. Past can truly become past, distinguished from present and future. Affects of serenity, joy, pleasure and excitement come into being. Narcissism may be transformed into humour, wisdom and the capacity to contemplate one's own impermanence.[16]

Pollock feels that psychotherapy rather than biochemical treatments may help the individual to achieve these states of serenity. There can be a collaboration with the – often younger – therapist, and the transference can be used to work through once again the problems of rivalry, envy, castration fear and the loss of the self.

This therapeutic relationship is of course enormously helped when the ageing individual can find age-appropriate activities which can be developed in a satisfactory manner. The capacity for creative work and satisfaction is universal, and better education would enable more of us to continue in the same way as many artists who have produced astonishing work into their 70s and 80s. A well-known example would be the Spanish artist Goya, who retired from the world and ensconced himself in a farmhouse known as the 'Quinta del Sordo' (coincidentally he had become stone deaf in his 40s as the result of an acute infection) and there painted the so-called 'black paintings'. These seem to encompass aspects of his inner world and are extraordinarily violent and frightening. Having worked out these phantasies –

which are also works of great and at times overwhelming artistry –
Goya was able to re-emerge into the world and painted works of
great simplicity and beauty such as 'The Milkmaid of Bordeaux'.

Indeed, the later work of many artists seems to demonstrate an
ability to reduce their subjects to the basics and to make
statements which are startling in their simplicity and power.
Similarly, I consider it no accident that in *The Tempest*, his last
complete play, Shakespeare should have contained the action
within the space of 24 hours, and that the themes of revenge,
sibling rivalry, life and death should have been worked out in that
time. In a paper on late-life creativity which I wrote a few years
ago, I suggested that the play represented a final abandonment of
illusion as a barrier against the inevitability of dying and an
acceptance of the reality of ending.[17]

Moreover, Pollock makes the essential point that the notion of
the mourning liberation process is not only one that involves the
creation specifically of works of art. As he says,

> ... some people who do not produce 'works' are more
> talented than those who do, and some creative people have
> little talent ... The creativity may be expressed in more
> personal ways – in creative dreaming, for example – or in
> creative living through a fulfilled life for oneself and for others.
> I think that here we can link up with all the possibilities of
> study and work in later life which should be available to older
> people.

A therapeutic encounter which may well illustrate this theme
concerns a woman aged 70 whom I shall call Mrs P.

Mrs P. was treated some years ago under my supervision by a
young therapist whom I shall call Ms Y., and had some 30 sessions
of dynamic psychotherapy with us. Mrs P. presented complaining of mood swings from despair to manic activity, loneliness,
panic attacks, vertigo, loss of energy and drinking bouts. These
symptoms were acutely manifested whenever her relationship
with one of her two married daughters became troublesome. Mrs
P. had been divorced for some years, and had made two suicidal
gestures within the last decade.

Ms Y. decided with my support that she would focus on Mrs
P.'s relationship with her daughters, who had recently said to her
that they were sick and tired of her behaviour and that there was

no question of her coming to live with them if her condition deteriorated even should she wish to do so. Physically, Mrs P. was not very well since she suffered from an advanced arthritic condition, vertigo, and 70 per cent blindness in one eye – physical problems which had impinged on her lifestyle and her independence. For Mrs P., ageing was equated with senility, and she would get into a panic when her various illnesses flared up; she was equally convinced that her intellectual abilities would quickly deteriorate.

On assessment we felt that Mrs P. was suffering from a personality disorder with marked narcissistic features. We considered that she had managed her emotional problems mainly through manic activity, which had worked well until recently when she and her daughters had begun to have many difficulties in their relationships.

We learnt that as a child Mrs P. had felt extremely restricted by her mother, who had insisted that she be educated at home until the age of eight, in order to protect her from the negative and destructive aspects of life with the aim of producing a genteel young lady. Her father is described as reserved and rather cold – she describes him as being a classic gentleman. Her mother had died of sclerotic dementia when she was aged 48, and her father died in his early 50s from an unexpected cardiac arrest – she had been able to mourn his death and had experienced great feelings of loss. A younger brother was homosexual and had committed suicide in his 20s.

Mrs P. described her background as typical English middle-class, which promoted an immature, perfectionistic personality type. In reaction to this she had developed a manic thirst for life and became involved in many political activities. She had married a man 11 years her senior (whom she described as being similar in character to her father) by whom she had two daughters. He divorced her after 16 years of marriage.

Mrs P. returned to university at the age of 62 and gained a degree. She secured part-time employment, took up squash for the first time and became a foster grandparent. She undertook these activities in addition to her enthusiasm for classical music and the theatre.

At interview we thought at length about her problems centering around her vulnerability and fear of rejection, and decided that her very complex and difficult relationship with her own mother had been the prototype for her later relationships. Despite her advanced years, she had a very tentative notion of self at this time.

We thought that she had now come to a transitional period in her life when her defences against commitment were being challenged. Her daughters, instead of being willing to act as extensions of herself, were in fact preferring to live their own lives, rather than give her the narcissistic supplies on which she felt so dependent. In this way, her feelings of panic, mood swings, and consumption of alcohol seemed to be a response to her need for close and intense relationships. She had no sense of ever having been able to master conflict, and had never had time for what she saw as 'the important things in life'.

In the therapy Mrs P. tried hard at first to keep matters on an intellectual level, rather than admitting to her needs for dependency and support. This was linked to the developmental failures which had never allowed her to separate properly from her mother: this problem was now being echoed by her daughters' refusal to play their assigned role with her. As a result she made considerable demands on her therapist for advice and support, and Ms Y. soon became aware of the feeling that she was having to act as a parent to her own parent. She was treated as if she was all good and had the power to magically satisfy Mrs P.'s needs. Any attempt to help her to find her own solutions or to show her that there were reality factors operative as well was dismissed with scorn.

Parenthetically, since Ms Y. was an attractive young woman in her late 20s, we wondered how far the patient would allow her an interpretative stance. However, it turned out that because this was a brief psychotherapy on the Malan model, and that therefore the boundaries of the therapeutic relationship were clearly defined from the beginning, Mrs P. allowed the therapist to 'assume' her preoccupations. In other words, she was able after the first few sessions to present a great deal of material, making her own links to the past when Ms Y. made interpretations about what was happening between them in the present. The therapist was felt to be holding Mrs P.'s preoccupations while she could explore past related material.

In the course of this therapy, Mrs P. became much less manic, drank less and became more contemplative. Her relationship with her daughters improved, and she lived more contentedly. Ageing became no longer equated with senility, and the pleasures of life could be accepted more passively. She became less overwhelming in her demands on her daughters and her therapist so that in her last session she could say to her, 'You don't know what it is like to be 70 – but you had some good ideas.'

In other words, quite a lot was achieved in some 30 sessions, although plainly there were problems which it had not been possible to address. The point here was that through her therapy Mrs P. had been able to address some lifelong problems and abandon her manic defences against some of her anxieties. This had led her to a far more creative solution to her recurrent problems, and also increased her capacity to tolerate the losses of ageing and the renunciation of some of her ideal phantasies about herself.

Another patient whom I would like to describe I shall call Jeffrey.

Jeffrey came to the clinic and said that he needed a psycho-analyst as he was in need of some urgent treatment. At that time he was 77, and was somewhat dirty, unshaved and unkempt. He suffered from an essential tremor of the hands which was familial. He was quite clear that what he wanted was to see a psychoanalyst and not a psychiatrist or a psycho-geriatrician. He was in good physical health, but complained of mild depression, excessive anxiety, and instability in human relationships. He added that these feelings were compounded by age, loneliness and a lifelong severe neurosis. He told me that he was a veteran of psycho-analysis, having had treatment with various of my colleagues between the wars. Unfortunately, I was not able to consult any of these colleagues since they were all deceased.

The reason for his original referral was a sexual difficulty, which became troublesome when he fell in love with a distin-guished woman, a lawyer who was at that time in analysis with Ernest Jones. Jones saw him in consultation at her request and referred him to a colleague. His difficulty was that he was extremely inhibited sexually, he masturbated continually and was constantly caught up in sexual fantasies and in some perversions in reality. He told me that they were very recondite and unusual perversions, although he never disclosed to me what they actually were.

Eventually Jeffrey became engaged to the woman, although when they tried to have intercourse she told him that his penis was not sufficiently stiff to satisfy her and subsequently broke off the engagement. To this day he remains puzzled and regretful about her rejection of him. He knows that she was unreasonable, since he later married a woman with whom he was able to be potent, although with some difficulty. However, when Jeffrey eventually fathered a son by her, he gave up sexual intercourse for good because his precocity had returned. Much of his life was devoted to bringing up this son.

In my interviews with Jeffrey, it emerged that the reason that he had sought help was the murderous rage that he felt towards his daughter-in-law. She is a Turkish woman whom his son married some years ago and they live in his house with him. Because of his tremor, he cannot cook for himself and thus he is very dependent upon her for hot food. She refuses to be helpful, having a fearful temper and he finds himself constantly in conflict with her. I took him into treatment, both in the hope that I could help him and because I was fascinated to work with a patient whose experience with some of the great names of the past in my profession would somehow link me with the heroic days of psychoanalysis before the Second World War.

Interestingly, Jeffrey began to dream copiously, and almost at once brought me a dream in which he was struggling with a scorpion, struggling on 'a great pile of shingle, writhing and moving on all fours'. I thought that he was here telling me of some of his primal scene phantasies, about a terrifying castrating scorpion woman, about not being able to stand and about the primal scene. His associations led him to memories of his childhood and two traumatic incidents which he felt had never emerged in his previous work. The first trauma was the birth of his brother and the second was the fact that his mother became pregnant. But this hatred for a younger sibling had never become the core of his previous analyses.

I made the link with his anger and hatred for his son at this time, and showed him how he needed me as a younger rival in the transference. This led to material about being bathed together with his brother and how he thought that his nanny had used to arouse him by manipulating his penis. Following this he had sexual fantasies in which the idea of being undressed and bathed by a young girl were very prominent. He was very surprised that such fantasies had never entered his mind before, even though there was a great deal of sexual material about. He was reminded, too, of the way in which his father would look at his mother – a look which he considered to be extremely sexual.

Other interesting and relevant material which emerged was that he felt himself to have been very hemmed in as a child, and remembers that he wore something called a 'binder' – a strap which tied up his penis and kept it in check. He says that, not surprisingly, he was very puzzled by this when he was young. He reports various fantasies when he was a boy about the rival strengths of father and mother, and wondering whether he and mother could overcome his stern and distant father. He felt that he might be able to fly, to hover about the ceiling where he would be out of danger and have power. He could remember sitting on a lavatory seat shouting for his mother. She took a long time coming which drove him frantic with misery and disappointment. He said that his childhood was really desolate, and when I asked him about this word said that it was just a feeling because everyone was so strict. He remembered hitting a nurse with a slipper when she was cutting his toenails. He was afraid that she would cut the wrong thing, so his father beat him – 'the bloody man'.

I pointed out to him how much he had hated his father and he replied that he was indeed aware of that. It was not difficult to see why since his father was always punishing him: he was a dreary person and showed such indifference to his sons. He and his brother played together but the brother too was a nuisance – they played but they quarrelled much more. Indeed, quarrelling seems to pursue him. He has a screen memory in which he remembers seeing a boy's arm caught in the wheel of a cart and that there was a lot of blood. I said that perhaps he wanted me to be a master analyst who could take away his fear of castration and all that it stood for. 'Oh, yes,' he said. 'I am more or less conscious of this. I am afraid of the excitement and fear the loss of control. I know that I have lots of hostility to women, but the castration anxiety makes it worse.'

I worked with Jeffrey for several years. I felt privileged to work with a survivor of the 1930s who seemed to have a considerable and, I thought, to some extent genuine grievance, that psycho-analysis had not helped him as much as he hoped that it would and that as a result his life had been a failure both sexually and professionally. As you might anticipate, an enormous amount of sexual and aggressive feeling emerged, with the key being an experience in which he burned the plump arm of a girl at a party with a cigarette. We worked out that this was a clear expression of his phantasy of sexual intercourse and explained why he had had such difficulties in being potent with women throughout his life. Clearly he feared not only what he might do to women, but also what they might do to him in retaliation.

Jeffrey complained very bitterly of the emptiness and sadness of his life, and of his wish to end it very soon. He had just about given up his compulsive masturbation when there was a re-crudescence when a young woman in a coffee shop smiled at him. He at once fell madly and idealistically in love with this young woman, whom he has never met again. He seeks her in the streets where he lives, goes to the coffee shop every week on the anniversary of their meeting, but has never had the good fortune to see her again. She obviously represents the idealized sexual object that he has been seeking for all his life and on whom so much of the hopes of a solution to his problem have been pinned. The other side of his problem is the Turkish daughter-in-law who treats him so badly and with whom he is compelled to carry on civil war.

What was my role as a therapist in all this? Jeffrey came to me essentially to find the opportunity of working through and finally laying his ghosts to rest. He needed help to give up at long last the massive denial involved in his fears of abandonment and desola-tion involved in his perverse fantasy situation, and to accept the inevitable – the contemplation of his own death, including the extinction of his own sexuality. He assigned me the role of organizer to help him rework his sexualized defences against his profound anxieties.

Psychoanalysts, who were after all supposed to be knowledge-able about sex, had always had a role in Jeffrey's life in providing him with an organized protection against his very primitive fears of loss and abandonment, which had emerged in the face of threats by his family to place him in a home for old people. He needed me to protect him from a fate which for him was truly worse than death. The phase-specific problem here was where he would live when he was abandoned finally by the child whom he had idealized, and on to whom he had projected the ideal and immortal parts of himself. This was the final insult and abandon-ment by his objects, and one which he needed me to help him find a fantasy to live by, rather than his perverse fantasies. I saw his fantasies as a defence against falling into nothingness – one of Winnicott's nightmare situations.

7
Death

It is interesting to note that until quite recently psychotherapists were reluctant to write at any length about death and dying. Partly this stemmed from the fact that initially patients tended to be in the age range between 25 and 40 years, and many therapists believed Freud's dictum that people over the age of 50 were unanalysable. I can remember when I started out in practice, that if an elderly man or woman presented to the adult department at the Tavistock Clinic and they seemed suitable for therapy, the response was that we had better send them to a Jungian, since they were interested in older patients and would be prepared to treat them. Pearl King's landmark paper on the treatment of older patients was first read at a Jungian Congress.[18] I myself only became interested in the work when I met George Pollock.

Various writers have contributed to changing our views on this matter, none more so than Irving Yalom, whose volume of studies on psychotherapy in later life is invaluable for the therapist.[19] Yalom is one of those rare therapists who is not afraid to look at the themes of death and dying, and his work is of great importance in this context. He says,

> . . . the reality of death is important to psychotherapy in two distinct ways: death awareness may act as a boundary situation and instigate a radical shift in life perspective, and death is a primary source of anxiety.

Yalom defines a 'boundary situation' as an event, an urgent experience, that propels one into confrontation with one's existential situation in the world. A confrontation with one's personal death – *my* death – is the *non pareil* boundary situation and has the power to provide a massive shift in the way that one lives in the world. The physicality of death destroys any feelings of immortality that the individual may hold. Let me try and illustrate this by an account of an AIDS patient whom I treated until his recent death.

Fisher, as I shall call him, was first referred to a physician colleague. He was infected with HIV which progressed to AIDS at the time when he had a serious bout of pneumocystis pneumonia, which complicated treatment for a Hodgkin's lymphoma. He experienced a near-death phenomenon, and recovered with no illusions about his potential mortality. Recent research suggests that patients with lymphoma and AIDS rarely survive more than a few months.

It is noteworthy that of all the AIDS patients of this particular London teaching hospital who have died, Fisher survived the longest after the diagnosis of AIDS. This, of course, does exclude those who may still survive, but on them I cannot comment. I wish here to give an account of the measures which we took to help him, and to lay particular emphasis on the psychological factors which we feel may have helped him to both live an acceptable life and achieve a 'good' death.

After his recovery from PCP, Fisher expressed a positive wish to live, and began a course of vitamin C therapy, involving three-times-a-week infusions, a chore as well as involving pain. As part of his treatment, Fisher was referred to me for psychoanalysis, and I undertook to see him initially on a twice-a-week basis during his visits to this country. The treatment followed the standard model, except that by Fisher's wish we sat in chairs facing each other. The main drive of the treatment was to help Fisher understand and try and deal with his existential situation, given that his immune system had been so badly damaged by his illness. Therefore, he had to deal with the overwhelming and imminent threat of death.

Both of us agreed that the first steps we might take were to engage in a review of Fisher's life and relationships in the hope of trying to understand and ameliorate something of his present problems of making sense of both his life and his inevitable death.

Fisher at this time was not resident in England and spent the greater part of the time engaged in building what we agreed to call a 'castle in Spain' – a house which would give him the possibility of realizing a personal dream in a fertile and warm part of the Iberian Peninsula where he could show the world the kind of creative and artistic person he felt himself to be. His previous attempts to do this had not been successful, insofar as he had begun a promising career in an artistic field but had eventually abandoned this career in order to live with his benefactor, 'Kay'.

Kay had set up house in East Anglia with Fisher, who gardened and kept house for him. They had lived together for some years in a fairly stable homosexual relationship, in the course of which it became clear both that Kay had contracted HIV and that he had infected Fisher. His role in Kay's life was to be an occasional partner and an adornment for his elegant life. During the later stages of Kay's illness, Kay became hypomanic, and was enormously demanding. Fisher nursed him through his terminal illness and by the end felt he had to ease Kay into death after weeks of suffering. At the commencement of the therapy Fisher recounted, without much affect, that he had finally suffocated Kay in order to reduce his agony. This attitude changed markedly as the therapy progressed.

Kay had been wealthy and had left Fisher enough money so that he no longer needed to work. He felt that he should try and escape his guilt by building his dream house, and in that way escaping the envy of Kay's friends and family. When Fisher had tried to circumvent his guilt about Kay's death, circumstances had stopped him from really achieving what he wanted, so that when he came to therapy he reported that his dominant feelings were those of depression.

Fisher's history was that he was the only son of a diplomat and a professional woman, who had been parted by circumstances to do with his father's work when he was five. His mother was described as extremely controlling and unloving, and had used the boy as an extension of herself so that he had never really had any sense of his own identity. Fisher had early discovered an artistic gift, and this had been encouraged by his mother between the ages of 5 and 10 when his father was in another country. He had thus escaped from his family into his artistic pursuits, and had begun to have some success in his career.

In discussing his gifts it came as something of a surprise to Fisher when it became clear that there was an unconscious agenda in his work, which had to do with his struggling with, controlling and overcoming his maternal imago through his art. While he was able to do this, what he did not achieve was satisfaction with what he created, which always remained the enemy which he had to conquer rather than an achievement in which he could take pride.

Given his history, it was perhaps no surprise that while at university he fell in with a homosexual group and quite rapidly came out. Fisher's relationship with Kay, who was the major figure in his life, was a rather sadomasochistic one in which he took a passive role, and coped with his lover's bursts of manic behaviour and at times compulsive sexual promiscuity.

The focus of the work in the psychotherapy was Fisher's wish to understand and ameliorate his existential situation, overcome his guilt about his new-found wealth, and to find a creative outlet, given his rather weak physical state and the relatively short time that he had left to live. He came to understand the need to repair his damaged internal objects, and was able to use the therapist as an enabling figure in the transference to begin to do this.

While he veered between somewhat manic acting out and depression, he could make no links with the local community, and he gradually came to grips with the phantasy of what his house represented. He decided that he had no real need for such a mansion, and that he would do better to complete the building work and then sell the house at the end of the summer after he had been able to entertain his friends there and enjoy a last golden time with them.

Fisher had thought of taking up painting in oils, but saw that it would take more time than he had available, and so decided to work with linocuts instead. He explored his relationship with his parents in his childhood, and, as a result, was able to find for the first time some measure of understanding and intimacy with his father, who was able to tell Fisher of his own griefs and disappointments, but never with his mother.

It should not be imagined that this was all plain sailing. Fisher often missed sessions, and there was a period when he fell in love in a completely unreal way with a friend of his partner, Luke. At this time he absented himself from the therapy and spent something of a wild time in another city, cutting himself off from both medical and psychological supports. He told me that this episode had made him feel safe, but only for a while. Eventually however, he returned to England with a clear understanding of his failing physical condition and took up the psychological therapy again. Fisher wished further to explore his inner life, and we had recommenced on a three-times-a-week basis when his terminal illness began. Despite his severe physical difficulties, I visited him regularly at home and in hospital, and the therapeutic work continued until Fisher was no longer able to speak or communicate because of a mid-brain tumour.

From the psychoanalytic point of view, the major work was based on the interpretation of very early anxieties from the oral stage of psychosexual development. It seemed clear that Fisher's mother had not been able to play with him and help him towards the creation of a transitional object that he could call his own. He seemed much more a child who had had to act out his mother's phallic wishes, and it seemed unlikely that he had ever been able to play freely. He had no proper outlet for the aggression which he clearly felt towards this forbidding maternal figure, and in our view he had had to turn this against himself and against the artistic material, which he literally had to overcome and internalize in his quest for artistic perfection. The therapy seemed to give him permission both to do this and to allow his father a greater place in his life as an enabling model for behaviour.

When he fell ill, Fisher needed very careful nursing and medical care, which was unstintingly provided both by his friend Luke and by his physician. While he was at times in great pain, he fought the illness very hard and seemed reluctant to give up. His physician felt that Fisher had a psychological task to complete before dying. After some time in hospital, during which he put his affairs in order and made his will, it was agreed that Fisher should be looked after at home. He went gradually downhill, and a few weeks before his death, gradually lost the power of speech because of a brain tumour. Nevertheless, he remained able to respond to care, and his last words to his physician were, 'I'm happy.'

It seems that the good care that Fisher had been receiving permitted him to regress to an early infantile state, where the loving attention of his friends, nurses and physician represented the good early experience which he had only partially experienced before. Being able to get in touch with this and to enjoy it even in the very enfeebled state in which he was before he died enabled him to complete the task of dying in a way which was felt to be fulfilling and not tragic by those who cared for him.

Not all the psychological task was fulfilled, however. Those who cared for him in his last illness experienced Fisher's mother as intrusive, involved only in her own world, and unable to identify with her son's developing experience in any but the most superficial way. This pattern intensified as he approached death in that she could only talk of her own experience of motherhood, rather than appreciate Fisher's needs and experiences. A week before Fisher's death she put intensive pressure on the physician to give him morphine, and could not understand Fisher's attendant's view that as he was not in pain and was aware of what was happening he should be allowed to die in his own time. This conflict between her and the physician was a most painful episode for all concerned, but Fisher in fact did die as he wished. We understand that since his death, Fisher's name has not been mentioned in her household.

Fisher's treatment involved a therapeutic regime which differed greatly from that usually offered to people with AIDS. The patient consciously sought help with his existential problems knowing that he had lived in a way that compromised his talent and his integrity. When freed by the death of his rich lover, Fisher was intensely controlling and controlled, narcissistic and unable to admit to his vulnerability. Nevertheless, even before he developed the lymphoma, he recognized the need for change.

Another singular factor in this case was the close collaboration between physician and therapist. There are remarkably few reports on psychoanalytic therapy with this group of patients, but in none of these is there any suggestion of the degree of communication between the two professionals that existed in this case. Certainly, in the case reported earlier by one of us a good result was achieved, but it was achieved in isolation from the physician and without the possibility of exploring many of the variables which make this case so striking.[20]

Usually, such therapy as is offered to AIDS patients has either been counselling or based upon a cognitive behavioural model. Most counsellors subscribe to an approach which, while recognizing the existential state of the patient, prefers to base itself on the management of anxiety, exhortation and the reinforcement of positive aspects of the individual's situation. A psychoanalytic approach, on the other hand, concerns itself inevitably with the transference and with transferential feelings concerning important early figures in the patient's life, so that anger, rage, hatred and jealousy as well as love and reparation are inevitably expressed and to some extent worked through in the therapeutic situation. It seems to us that when he came into treatment, Fisher's identity depended largely on a retreat from his talent, the sadomasochistic use of money and an unremitting narcissism. When these were tackled with him, he was enabled to express the more vulnerable but far more positive aspects of himself.

It is always challenging to the medical profession when one of their patients, particularly those with a grave prognosis, throws away the medicines, takes to the hills and returns strong. What was particularly challenging about this case was that while Fisher worked through psychoanalysis to discover the ability to discover his real self, his physical health also showed remarkable recovery.

This case may help to persuade us to begin to reconsider our views on the nature of healing and on the mind-body relationship. Perhaps it is not enough to talk of mood in terms of depression, and so on; rather that we need to be more thoughtful about the deeper needs of the human personality. This may apply to a wide range of illnesses in which expensive treatment is applied impersonally and the psychosomatic element of the illness is missed. That this patient, with a viral infection, appeared to have a striking remission after facing internal conflicts and resolving them suggests that there would be value in exploring the role of mind in other illnesses.

The role of the psychoanalyst, and his or her way of writing up case histories representing months and years of intensive work, may well be difficult for those responsible for resource allocation to accept. That this patient's life was transformed by his therapy is clear, that he lived for four years instead of six months was remarkable, and in this time the medical contributions were minimal. It is of course possible that his medical costs would have been greater without the psychological input. Perhaps this should not be the only criterion: Fisher used the limited time left to him to determine his own identity in a way which was healing for his body and which affected those around him in a striking way. He could begin to discover the potentiality of trust in letting go of his various disguises, and his final regression into death was therefore enabled to be peaceful. He found in his physician a mother who could provide him with a true 'holding environment', within which he could regress and pick up the losses of his formative years. This new experience was fought out all around the patient without him necessarily being aware of it, as when his mother wished the physician to end his life. The physician's refusal, and her feeling that in possibly giving way to the mother she might cause Fisher to be suffocated rather than be allowed to die in his own way and in his own time, led to a very moving experience of his death shared by those who were present when he took his last peaceful breath.

When reporting this case we said that no one can counter the inevitability of death, with its dreaded disintegration of both the soma and the psyche. Nevertheless, treatment along these lines suggested by our work with this patient poses the question of the possibility of understanding better, as well as working with, the process of dying as a stage of psychic integration of early infantile experiences which may have had to be resisted or denied throughout life.

Yalom insists that for most of us the recognition of the reality and inevitability of one's own personal death is not easy. In his studies of people who are suffering from terminal cancers he gives many illustrations of the defences which we all use to try and deny the inevitability of our own death. He pays a great deal of attention to the ways in which many people try to deny the ageing process, which of course underlies the progress towards death of which we have been unconsciously aware all during our lives. He says,

> . . . the belief in personal specialness is extraordinarily adaptive and permits us to emerge from nature and to tolerate the accompanying dysphoria: the isolation, the awareness of our smallness and the awesomeness of the external world, of our parents' inadequacies, of our creatureliness, of the bodily functions which tie us to nature and most of all of the knowledge of death which rumbles unceasingly at the edge of consciousness . . .

> he goes on to quote the American poet Robert Frost who wrote, 'Forgive, O lord, my little jokes on Thee, And I'll forgive Thy great big one on me.'[21]

Among the defences which Yalom describes are compulsive heroism, workaholism and narcissistic involvement in oneself and one's own life experiences. Baudelaire described the artist as being all at one and the same time his own god, his own prophet and his own priest – a situation which will enable the artist to defy the fates and produce for himself as an individual.

I think that it will be clear that as we age we try and maintain our defences against the inevitable deterioration of our own bodies. Yet the brute facts of decline cannot be ignored by any one of us. For some people, a group or an individual psychotherapeutic situation can ease the painful process of accepting one's own mortality and the fact of one's personal extinction. In other cultures, the period of later life is one in which the individual retires from the world and devotes himself to the cultivation of the spiritual life and his relation to the Universal. In our culture I cannot help feeling that we tend towards various forms of denial which have a neurotic base, and, which though they may help in the short run, in the long run perhaps hinder the way in which we approach and accept the inevitability of our own deaths. Nothing in this area of our lives fails as completely as success.

What Yalom's patients who were struggling with coming to terms with their own existential problems said to him was essentially that they were appalled once they had recognized and become reconciled to their fate to see how completely they had been governed by their defences, and how little they had appreciated their own true needs and interests. Their experience was that many aspects of their lives which they had formerly felt to be essential, such as social position, work matters and so forth, had now lost all importance for them, and that they prized the opportunities for warmth and intimacy with those close to them.

I feel that the considerations which I outlined earlier in the book become essential for us as we approach death, and that we regress towards the reworking in a different key of the anxieties of early infancy. Thus where the infant is terrified of falling-into-nothingness or disintegrating into pieces in the face of an unknown and troubling world, and needs the help of a facilitating environment to provide him or her with reassurance and a feeling of personal safety, so the older person who is facing his own death needs to go back and confront the same problems in a different mode – indeed, in some ways a more frightening mode since there is no such thing as personal survival after death. In the face of the inevitable, which may involve pain, loss and the extinction of all that makes us who we are, we have to relearn, or, more often, learn for the first time, ways in which we can internalize and be comforted by the closeness and love of others.

This attitude is epitomized for me by Martin Grotjahn, an American colleague who wrote a few years ago about his own near-death experiences. He said,

For many years I had great expectations of old age. In my fantasies I would be wise, perhaps somewhat detached from the worries of this world, beyond desire and temptation, without frustration and therefore without anger. Finally I would be without guilt, without obligations and duties – just alive. That would be true freedom: freedom from inner drive and outer threat. I thought that as an old man I would finally be what I was supposed to be: I, myself and free.[22]

Grotjahn then recounts suffering a serious heart attack at the age of 80, which he at first tried to dismiss and refused to accept the diagnosis. It was only after a second even more serious heart attack that he finally accepted that after a long and extremely active and vigorous professional life, that he was in fact old. He suffered from angina and overwhelming anxiety attacks. He says, 'It was a panic without visual images, far beyond any words'. He records that other important people in his life took his illness seriously, so that he too was compelled to do so. He continues,

I live quite in comfort, but now definitely like an old man. Peculiarly enough I feel alright about it . . . I feel free from guilt . . . the guilt that goes with the feeling of never being as good as one ought to be to help someone. Let other people worry now. I am through with work and worry. I am a free man.

I sit in the sun watching the leaves fall slowly . . . I think, dream, sit and draw. I feel almost free of this world of reality. Whoever told me that I would be quietly happy just sitting here, reading a little, writing a little, and mostly enjoying life in a quiet and modest way, I would, of course, have not believed. That a walk across the street to the corner of the park would satisfy me more than a long walk, when only two years ago I thought that a four-hour walk was just not enough – that surprises me.

I have time now. I do not know how much time is left to me to live, but I am in no hurry. I am in no hurry to get anywhere, not even to the end of time. That can wait. When the time comes, I will try and accept it. I have no illusions; it will not be easy.

Right now I live in the moment, and I want to sit here a little while longer, quietly and hoping not to sit in anyone's way.

I always thought old age is an achievement in itself. I now know better; to get sick and live on, that is an achievement.

When I came home from the hospital, I had become old. My wife smiled at me and said, 'I have adopted you.' It is this kind of tender love I needed, and to which I tried to respond in kind. To have that kind of love makes us both happy. Life becomes worth living all over again when such tenderness is the final renewal.

8
Loss

No one will disagree with the notion that ageing involves a whole series of losses. We have to accept the fact that all our skills and physical abilities gradually decline, and that as we age we become less and less able to maintain the abilities which we had in the decade and a half between 15 and 30.

It is noteworthy that this is more painful for us than it was for previous generations, for whom adulthood and maturity were desirable and often admirable traits. It was not for nothing that Bismarck said after the Berlin Conference, which involved some very strenuous negotiations and redrew the map of Europe, that 'Das ist der Mann: der alte Jude'. It was clear that the man of the match had been Disraeli, the old Jew, whose skill, patience and tenacity had dominated the Conference. This attitude would be unlikely to be repeated today when the capacity to understand and use new technology is so crucial in so many ways to the life situation with which we must deal.

Let me try and spell out some of the losses which are inevitable and which we can do little to deny: physical inability, the gradual slowing down of mental processes, sexual incapacity and physical illness. It makes quite an imposing list. At the same time we will be working through the gradual acceptance of the increasing mortality of our parents if they have survived into our adulthood, and the problems associated with caring for them as they age. For many of us, this is far and away the most difficult part of the Third Age – watching those whom we first knew in their strength and sureness of being gradually deteriorating, and having to come to grips with their new dependence on us. I think that it is very hard for many people to accept that the strong father of their childhood is now an unhappy old man who has had a stroke and no longer has the capacity to manage his own affairs, or that the mother who was provider and omni-competent now has such bad arthritis that she can no longer cook for herself.

One of my patients who spent most of her childhood in India recently saw a new film about life in the sub-Continent and decided that she must take her mother to see it, because of its interest and the way in which it depicted some aspects of Indian life which she found absolutely fascinating. She put herself and her mother of 80 to some trouble to see the film, only to be very disappointed when her mother went to sleep after 10 minutes and found little of interest in the film when finally she awoke. She said sadly to me that she should have remembered that her mother's life had been largely in the cantonments of the British Army (her father had been a colonel) and that she now realized that although she found Indian culture of great interest, her mother's interests had centred much more round the golf course and the social life of the Anglo-Indian community. Her idealization of her mother and her projection of her own interests on to her had meant that what had been planned by her as a treat had been quite inappropriate.

Another patient with an elderly mother was terribly upset when after her flat had been burgled, her mother paid cursory interest to her loss, and instead insisted on reciting for the umpteenth time the story of her own burglary some 10 years before.

The vicissitudes of our early relationships will colour our later relationships with our ageing parents in every possible way. We often find ourselves in the position of wanting them to remain as powerful and omniscient as they were in our childhoods, while at the same time wanting to enjoy our own freedom and not to be dominated by them and by their needs. The intervention of the state has not helped here, since for so many the fact that it will supply an old people's home for their dependent relatives offers them the chance to avoid the working through of their feelings and attitudes to their parents in their later years. Nor is the problem helped by the narcissism and self-absorption of the parents themselves. I think here of King Lear and Lear's seeming abdication of power to his daughters – an abdication which is predicated on their continuing to pay him the respect that he feels he deserves and which denies his actual physical and psychological ageing. So often Cordelia's reply of 'Nothing' is the only one which we can make to the demands that the aged make upon us, since this of course is the only honest answer which is available to us.

All this makes tremendous demands upon the loving and reparative aspects of us all. We have to be aware of and accept the ageing process in ourselves while watching an accelerated version in our parents, and deal with it in terms of our own psychopathology. When our parents come to die, then we have to accept our losses and accommodate them within the framework of our now having become the adult generation and the next ones in line for death. We have to mourn and triumph in our own survival at one and the same time. I have known patients who felt that they had never truly begun to live until after the deaths of their parents, so hampered did they feel by their achievements and position in the world. But this is really not appropriate, since we all of us internalize parents from the very beginning of our lives and these internalizations remain with us for good.

One patient, whom I shall call Alan, came to me because he was tremendously troubled by memories of a former girlfriend whom he had offended in some minor way some 20 years before. Although, like the author of *Le Grand Meaulnes*, after his one brief meeting with Françoise he had never seen her from that day to this, whenever he became stressed in his difficult job with a power company, he would begin to obsess about their last meeting and the things that he felt that he should have said to her at that time which would have had the desired effect of making her respect and love him, rather than demonstrating her indifference for him.

Despite the fact that he was happily married and had two children upon whom he doted, this obsession was ruining his life. We worked together on this problem for some months, and in the course of the therapy spent some time trying to understand his childhood.

The only child of a naval family of some distinction, his father and mother had been distant and uncommunicative in the extreme. He had been sent off to the worst sort of English preparatory school at the age of eight, and from there to a religious institution where his sole recourse was to creep into the organ loft and weep the tears which otherwise could not be communicated to masters or to boys. Shy and self-effacing, he had not been allowed to go to university, and had to make do with going to a technical college.

Alan's life had been governed by shame, and his experience of women had not been very great when he met the young lady with whom he was so obsessed. He had hoped to impress her by organizing a party, only to find that the people whom he had wanted to invite were not able to come because he had chosen a date which clashed with an important college event. His female friend he felt had despised him because of what he felt to be his ineptitude, and as a result had refused his attempts to spend time with her after this, sending back his letters and other communications. (I thought that she was a rather inadequate young woman who did not know how to deal with a young man who was so overwhelmingly involved with her.)

It transpired as we began to work through Alan's obsession that the real reason for his difficulty lay in the fact that he could never feel valued in anything that he did by either of his parents, and that in order to keep them in his mind as the good and loving people whom they were not, he had to displace his feelings of shame and unworthiness on to the girlfriend who had disappointed him in such an unhappy manner so long ago. He had never until he entered therapy been able to really consider his negative feelings for his parents, but once he was able to do this he could begin the gradual process of freeing himself from his obsession. The resolution of this sad little tale was predicated upon his being able to begin to recognize his intense need and desire to be recognized and loved by the parents of his childhood, who were of course long dead, and finally deal with their inability to love and value him.

These are losses which we all have to come to terms with, and we have to learn to accept that not only are we not going ever to get the unconditional love and valuation which we experienced in our own childhoods ever again, but that the losses from that time will have to be sustained and worked with over long periods of time. I think that this demand is indeed capable of being sustained, and that the losses of the mid-life period can be worked with and can lay the foundation of new growth and change in our relationships.

David was the elder son of an extremely successful businessman who had spent most of his youth avoiding responsibility, living alone in a flat, drinking a great deal and smoking quantities of marijuana. He was able once we had begun to sort out his fear of rivalry with his father, and his enormous anger with him, to devote himself to the children of his own marriage in a way which his father had been unable to do, and to make a career in television as a writer and producer.

One other patient who illustrates well this question of loss would be a 55-year-old man whom I have called Socrates. An authority in his own field, he sought my help because of an inexplicable phobia about opening letters. Although he had never before sought help, he had developed a severe anxiety state, and feared that he would be pursued and put into gaol by the authorities.

Socrates came originally from Greece, the only son of a ship's captain and a cultivated society woman. His mother had not wished to spend much time with him; his childhood was spent with his many relatives in the various islands of the archipelago. When his mother subsequently had a daughter who died in early childhood, Socrates was made to feel responsible. Yet although we might have expected him to become withdrawn and schizoid, he enjoyed his childhood, having related well to his many relatives, particularly to an old couple who spoke to him in the local dialect and recognized and encouraged his already outstanding intelligence. One of his earliest memories, from about age six, concerned an arrangement to meet his mother at a particular café and have an ice cream with her. He arrived on time only to see his mother ride by in the family limousine and go off on a jaunt with a female cousin without him.

His parents emigrated to this country between the wars, and he was able to pursue a brilliant career in medicine. Unfortunately, like his namesake, he had married a shrew, a brilliant Classical scholar who also came from a Greek background who created for him a life which eventually became a living hell. His Xanthippe was determined to fail in whatever she did, while at the same time carping continually at him and denigrating everything that he had achieved. When I first knew him, their children had grown up and had thankfully left home, while Socrates lived a dog's life, shopping, cooking, cleaning and looking after Xanthippe, who had become quite maniacal in her constant attacks upon him, to the point where she refused to allow him a desk let alone a study in their home. All his papers and books had to be kept at work, and if he wished to write for a learned journal he would write papers in his head and dictate them in final draft to his secretary.

As we worked together, it became clear that the precipitating factor in his anxiety state was the death of Xanthippe's mother many years before. While Socrates and his wife were away on a family holiday with the children, the old lady had stayed in their house. She had fallen asleep while smoking a cigarette and had died in the subsequent fire which had devastated their house. Xanthippe naturally blamed him for her mother's death despite the fact that they had been over a thousand miles away at the time, and continually and relentlessly punished him, with protest or retaliation on his part. We gradually came to understand that the official letters were feared because they might contain invitations to go abroad again, with the consequence that there might be another death. It took longer for him to see that the death in question was that of his wife.

After some months of treatment he had a healing dream in which he vividly experienced a feeling of redness. We came to understand that this was a preverbal representation of his intense anger towards the women in his life, of rage towards his mother and his wife. In the transference, I was positively identified as a (returned) father who had helped him work through his feelings by giving him a language through which to express them. I identified the ways in which his altruism punished him and showed him the secret destructive rage which lay beneath all that he did for his wife and to a lesser extent for others. Over time he was able to become more overtly aggressive with Xanthippe, to take appropriate steps when she attacked him physically, and to arrange for psychiatric help when she threatened suicide or appeared to be on the verge of a new psychotic breakdown. His symptom became less disabling and he lost some of his fear of the authorities.

One of the most striking qualities displayed by Socrates was his great skill as a teacher. He had an extraordinary capacity to develop ideas in others often at the expense of his own. He was enjoyable for me to work with, not merely because he was a highly intelligent and cultured man, but because I found that I could do my work in an extremely satisfying way. He had the capacity to enable me to draw on hitherto unsuspected and imaginative creative aspects of myself which led me to think of new ideas and approaches to familiar problems. I suggested to him that it seemed that he was operating a profound split in which he assumed all the badness in intimate situations, while projecting the creative parts of himself into me and into his colleagues and students.

As we worked on this notion, his life changed even further. Until this time I understood that he never slept more than four hours a night, waking to listen to the World Service of the BBC every morning at 4 am. Now he began to sleep through the night, to assert himself more, to be less reliant on alcohol, while he gradually lost the marked depressive features which had underlain his anxiety state, and which he had never acknowledged to anyone before. The most rewarding change came in his view of his own work. Socrates had regarded himself as a burnt-out volcano, with no more ideas of substance to offer. But he suddenly began to write papers which offered revolutionary perspectives on his chosen field, moving into a late-life creative period which was deeply satisfying to him. Although he knew that he would never leave Xanthippe, and must therefore accept that he would probably never have the opportunity for a really loving and sensual relationship with a woman, life now really held meaning for him. Proud of his achievements, his own man, he could at last begin to overcome his early losses and enjoy new gratifications such as pride, fame, travel and his grandchildren. In Erikson's sense, he moved towards wisdom and personal integrity.

It is also common for many women who have had the experience of having to deal with inadequate and depressed mothers during infancy, so that they have had to be, as Maggie Mills has pointed out, 'mothers to their own mothers' to need to come to terms with this difficulty in their later life and be able to cope with their own children in a positive and creative way. This problem becomes quite acute as the mothers age, and it is often vital for psychotherapeutic help to be provided at the point where the depressed mother begins to age and to really become dependent on her daughter, who by this time may well have children and a family of her own and more pressing needs than those of an ageing parent with which to deal. One would really need to write a book on the vicissitudes of the mother-daughter relationship in later life, and curiously it is not one which has been dealt with at great length either in the literature of psychoanalysis or in literature generally. While mother-son relationships are well documented, both in literature and in politics – with Mrs Gandhi and her sons and Mrs Thatcher and the series of glossy young cabinet ministers whom she seems to have invested with a sublimated Oedipal capacity – the relationships between women and their daughters have not received the same treatment.

I think that it is accepted as a given that the mothers will be supportive and loving and will gladly take on the role of grandmothers and carers for the grandchildren. Of course it is not like that at all. I have a very clear memory of one woman who complained bitterly that when she was just about to give birth to her first child, her mother promptly went into hospital in order to have an operation for haemorrhoids. Her mother was a very narcissistic woman who had abandoned her child to foster-parents when she was five, and although she had taken her back when she was 12, she had never been able to accept the need to play a proper maternal role during her adolescence and early adulthood.

Fortunately, the patient had married a loving and supportive husband who was able to help her make good some of the mothering which she had missed out on in her early years, and who was able to give their children a modicum of parental care. Yet it turned out in later life that the children were to some degree neglected, and the first child of this particular woman expressed something of her deprivation by becoming a lesbian and finding in an older woman the mothering and care of which her own mother had been deprived and had not really been able to give to her own children.

While we all have to deal with the loss of our own parents as we age, what has a fairly rare but nevertheless crucial impact on later life is the loss of children. A visit to any country churchyard will confirm you in the understanding that up until the First World War the incidence of infant and child mortality was appalling, and that an enormous proportion of children died in the first decade of life. For us, with the advantages of modern medical knowledge, such a mortality rate is unthinkable. But when we do lose children either in infancy or as adults, the effect is almost unthinkable in modern terms. I remember talking to the late Geoffrey Gorer, who was one of the few modern British sociologists to consider the phenomena of death and dying seriously, and we agreed that the death of an adult child was in a sense an irretrievable wound. I have worked with several patients who have lost children either in accidents or as the result of a successful suicide, and I have no doubt that they were never able to recover from the trauma which the loss represented.

I think first of Helga, a 55-year-old social worker who was referred to us shortly after the suicide of her only child, a son of 21. He had been assessed by us a year earlier and found unsuitable for outpatient psychotherapy, and referred to a psychiatric unit. A student of dentistry, he had 'blown his mind with LSD'. I suspect that he was in fact schizophrenic. When Helga was seen by one of our consultants, she told him that her despair and depression were irremediable. She wished only to commit suicide, and would do so once her son's affairs were cleared up. He told her that we would not attempt to prevent her doing so, but that she should have the opportunity if she wished to work with me on her problems in the meantime.

Helga was born to a wealthy family in Eastern Europe. After both parents had been killed by the Nazis, she had spent her adolescence in the Resistance. After the war she came to England and married a man who was much older than herself, who had died some 18 months earlier. Helga had had a good career in the social services, and had become an acknowledged expert on the treatment of battered children. Her life had been bound up with her hopes for her intelligent only son, who carried her hopes for a brilliant career. With his death she felt that she had little or nothing left to live for. I could see that to try and help Helga, she and I would have to confront some appalling experiences if we were to get behind the main defences and face her depression. We worked together for about six months, and were sometimes able to link her loss with the terrible losses of the war-time period.

Given the possibility of her committing suicide, I always made sure that there was cover available during my holidays, and during Christmas the consultant who had originally assessed her saw her in my absence. She wound up her son's affairs and in fact killed herself on New Year's Eve. She left a note for the coroner, absolving me and the consultant of any blame. We had tried hard to help her, she said, but she had decided that she no longer wished to live.

It was clear that her son represented her immortality, and that with his death she no longer wished to live. I certainly could not offer her much in the way of hope, or do much more than try and contain and help her express her overwhelming feelings of loss. I felt that I could try and share her life review and concentrate on trying to help her feel that there was some value in her life and her work for others. I was prepared, I thought, to go through her horrors with her if she wished me to. She left me no option but to accept her final choice, and perhaps do her the small service of containing my own anger at her destruction of the attempts at creative work which we had made together and accepting her retaliation for the loss of her objects and the way in which life had treated her.

Another patient whom I have briefly referred to in a previous chapter was Mr W., a policeman in his 50s. He complained of depression, stress and psychosomatic symptoms following the death of his older son in a motorcycle accident.

The patient described himself as having been brought up in Scotland in the depression in a rather impoverished family. He had had a rather deprived childhood in a lower-middle-class family with all the restrictions that that involved. He had found a way out by joining the navy when he was 18. After his service, he became a policeman because he enjoyed the street work and what he called 'the involvement and excitement on some occasions and the patience required on others.' He married young because his wife was pregnant. The relationship was almost immediately unhappy, but this couple continued to live under the same roof for many years despite the absence of both sexual and social intercourse. For Mr W. this 'open' marriage became entirely comfortable for him. He had no interests at home apart from repairs and carpentry, and his social life was almost entirely outside the home in the physical activities which he most enjoyed.

His consultation centred round the traumatic effect on him of the death of his older son three years before. He had trained his son to be an expert. The day before the boy's death, he had seen that he was carrying out a repair on his bike by himself. My patient had had the money in his pocket to pay for the required part, but had decided that it would be more character-building to let the boy do the job by himself. The next day Victor had been out riding when the repair had failed and he had been killed in the subsequent crash. Mr W. had gone to the hospital where he had been taken and had stayed with him until he had died. He had always blamed himself for his son's death. Later in the same year he had been called to the same hospital in the middle of the night because his second son had had an accident in his car. The boy had lost control and gone head-first through the windscreen of his car and his face had been badly lacerated.

He had also suffered a third loss, a girl who was at that time in her late 20s, she seemed very much a homosexual love object, 'a Valkyrie with blonde hair and a powerful bike, who looked great in her leathers'. When she left him for a much younger man he became enraged and threatened her and her new boyfriend with physical violence.

Mr W. presented himself as a very sensitive, understanding and thoughtful man who seemed to be working in a job far beneath his real physical capacities. He seemed to be well in touch with his feelings and was able to tell me that in his view he was suffering from a mid-life crisis related to guilt and suffering over the death of his son. He had based his life on a manic defence against depression which had been augmented by what Balint has called a philobatic behaviour in various important areas of his life. He had come for help because these defences had been disrupted by the death of his son and the desertion of the girlfriend, who had obviously taken his place. His panic feelings seemed to be very much the result of an intense conflict between aggression towards his lost objects and a wish to preserve them. It seemed that if I were to help him he would need to ventilate something of the guilt and grief connected with his son's death, which would enable him to be much freer to deal with his other life problems.

Originally, I took Mr W. on for a brief therapeutic contract which centred on the themes which I have outlined. There were difficulties, however, since he was very well defended, full of aggression and felt that to show me his feelings, and particularly his grief, would make him look girlish in front of me. As part of his denial he had learned to fly, and he would try and ignore his feelings and rehearse the actions which one uses in landing an aeroplane. This fear of loss of control included angry feelings as well. The patient felt his aggression and strength to be extremely dangerous to those around him. He treated me at times as a superior officer and was suprised that I could be human and tolerant. He felt that this was all wrong since in my place he would not have behaved in such a way. He threatened me at times with physical assault if I did or said something which was unacceptable. I was at times quite frightened of him.

I left on a holiday at the end of our therapy, and when I returned, there were messages to say that he wished to see me again. He had suffered from an acute depression and blind panic attacks during my absence, and his medical advisers were at their wits' end to know what to do about him. His GP wrote me saying, 'I would like him under St Thomas' Hospital with the ECT machine fully charged. I would not like to cross this man; he is physically strong and could well kill someone in a rage.' I therefore took him back into treatment and he was placed in charge of the communications room of his local police station, where his need to control everything found a very constructive and acceptable outlet.

From this time on the work focused on a problem which is

often very central in the lives of ageing men and women, viz., giving up an omnipotent control over the lives of those around them and accepting the passive giving and generous aspects of their own natures. For Mr W. this led to a massive state of confusion – on the one hand, he still felt the need to control everything and everybody, particularly me, and on the other hand could he ever trust anybody, particularly me. Just before Christmas of that year he brought me a Christmas card with a cartoon of Santa Claus sitting on a chimney pot with his trousers down. I interpreted that this exemplified his attitude towards those to whom he offered his generosity.

After some time in therapy, things began to change and my patient became much softer and gentler in his relationships with those around him. He was able to talk more about his wife, who had up to now been an almost completely anonymous figure. He began to make plans to divorce her – she was quite capable of managing on her own as well as applying for retirement from the force. He also planned to undertake a course of study in a field which interested him.

Things seemed to be moving towards a point where we could begin to envisage the ending of the therapy when he telephoned me in great distress saying that he had to see me. When we met, he told me that his surviving son had had what seemed to be a schizophrenic episode while decorating a friend's cottage in the countryside. He had immediately dashed there, fearful that the boy had committed suicide. He discovered however that the boy had merely wandered off and had been picked up by the local police and taken to a mental hospital. Mr W. persuaded the psychiatrists to discharge him and brought him home.

This son, whom I shall call Abel, felt that machines were destroying the world and that we should all return to nature. He began by attacking his own parents' house and garden where he caused much destruction and then began to wrench mirrors off the motor cars of their neighbours, and leaving a trail of other damage through the village where they lived, so that he was arrested and sent to a prison hospital for observation. During this time, Mr W. maniacally repaired the damage that he had caused, but then had to accept that there was little or nothing that he could do to ameliorate the situation. In our work at this time we had to re-enact his unresolved grief over his older son's death and his inability to do anything about that as well. We did what we could in the therapy, which certainly was a genuine and helpful experience for him at this time.

Over the next year, things went from bad to worse: Abel continued ill, smashing up his parents' home so that his father had to call in his own colleagues and charge him. He spent three months in prison on remand and then was sent to the local mental hospital on remand. He seemed to have stabilized, and we hoped that at long last things might settle down. Then, when I was away in another country on a lecture tour, Abel too was killed – by a railway train after he had broken out of the hospital. On my return, my patient, who had not been in touch with the clinic, came into my room and said simply, 'Abel is dead.' He then recounted the events of this terrible tragedy, his agony and fury with the authorities, the funeral and his reactions, but all in a completely distant and unemotional manner. I did what I could to help him express his grief and pain, his guilt and his rage, but he still would not allow himself to cry with me. The most effective intervention that I made was to suggest that he go and see the film *Ordinary People*, about the reaction of a family to the death of an adolescent son. He did go with a woman friend who cared about him. She was able to hold him all night while he wept for his lost sons. Although he could tell me of this experience and be grateful to me for helping him acknowledge its importance, he could never allow himself to have the same sadness and despair with me.

The final chapter in this story of despair and desolation came when his wife, about whom he now felt guilty and responsible, became seriously ill with renal failure and needed a kidney transplant. Despite this she eventually died of renal cancer and he had to cope with yet another loss. I fully expected him to make some sort of manic flight, but instead he retired to the south coast, where at first to my relief he seemed to have managed to have constructed as good a life as one might have hoped for him. I have described what in fact happened and how he took flight into a most unhappy marriage in an earlier chapter.

There is one other person whom one should mention in discussing the concept of irreparable loss. Sigmund Freud lost his beloved daughter Sophie in the epidemic of Spanish influenza at the end of the First World War. Writing to Ferenczi to inform him of the death of Sophie he added, 'As for us? My wife is quite overwhelmed. I think: *La Science Continue*. But it was a little much for one week.' Writing to the helpful Eitingon somewhat later, he described his reaction: 'I do not know what more there is to say. It is such a paralysing event, which can stir no after-thoughts when one is not a believer and so is spared all the conflicts that go with that. Blunt necessity, mute submission.'[23] Jones adds:

... in the same month something happened that had a profound effect on Freud's spirits for the rest of his life. His grandchild, Heinerle, Sophie's second child had been spending several months in Vienna with his Aunt Mathilde. Freud was extremely fond of the boy, whom he called the most intelligent child whom he had ever encountered. He had had his tonsils removed about the time of Freud's first operation on his mouth, and when the two patients met after their experiences he asked his grandfather with great interest 'I can already eat crusts, can you?' Unfortunately the child was very delicate, 'a bag of skin and bones' having contracted tuberculosis in the country the previous year. He died of miliary tuberculosis, aged four and a half on June 19th. It was the only occasion in his life when Freud was known to shed tears. He told me afterwards that this loss had affected him in a different way from any other which he had suffered. They had brought about sheer pain, but this one had killed something in him for good. The loss must have struck something peculiarly deep in his heart, possibly reaching even as far back as the little Julius of his childhood. A couple of years later he told Marie Bonaparte that he had never been able to get fond of anyone since this misfortune, merely retaining his old attachments: he had found the blow quite unbearable, much more so than his own cancer. In the following month he wrote to say that he was suffering from the first depression of his life, and there is little doubt that this may be ascribed to that loss, coming so soon as it did after the first intimations of his own lethal affliction. Three years later, on consoling with Binswanger whose own eldest son had died, he said that Heinerle stood for all children and grand-children. Since his death *he had not been able to enjoy life*: he added 'It is the secret of my indifference – some people call it courage – towards the danger to my own life.'

The anger, pain and incredulity that have to be faced when one is considering one's own death present the individual with as much of a problem as does the notion of a parental intercourse that excludes him or her. It may well be that just as the acceptance of the notion of an exclusive intercourse may release creativity and foster independent thinking, so acceptance of death, of the reality of one's own end and one's own extinction may curtail the ordinary omnipotence of thought from which we all suffer and promote, what Erikson in his account of the life cycle has called integrity at the expense of despair.

I have tried to show throughout this book that older people are remarkably easy to work with in the therapeutic situation, but my experience does suggest a caveat as far as the special group who have lost children are concerned. As I see it these people have suffered a narcissistic wound that never can be healed. Instead of being able to hand on the best parts of themselves to their descendants, they have had to accept a real caesura – a break in the chain that in psychological terms is irreparable. Although the patient may be parent, love object or child in the transference, it seems that there is no way in which we can help the patient restore and repair the lost object of his or her projections and idealizations when the child actually dies. Even for those whose children go mad, there is still the hope that one day they will regain their sanity. But where there is no hope, we have to accept that all that might potentially have been there can no longer be. It seems to me that those who have suffered the losses which I have just described throw into relief the problems that face the rest of us –the reality of our own deaths.

| Afterword

I have tried in this book to present a psychodynamic point of view on the question of age and ageing in our present Western society. I have left out ways in which other cultures regard and treat ageing, since that would have given the book a rather different dimension than the one which in fact I have taken. I have throughout the book taken the view that ageing is a process which is worthy of study and understanding in its own right and that the too easy equation of adulthood and then senescence as developmental stages should now be abandoned and a more thoughtful view taken by those whose job it is to work with older people.

If there is any lesson to be learned from this work, then it must be the enormous richness and variety of the ageing process and how much the Third Age has to offer us. I once had a phantasy about what I would do once I had retired, provided I had the health and the resources to allow me to do what I wanted. I decided that I would go to Germany for a year and study German – I have a reasonable gift for languages – so that I might have the pleasure of reading Freud in the original. After that I decided I would look for an old house in Italy and spend most of my time there, rebuilding the house and writing various books that I have never had time to begin because of my professional commitments. I hoped that my children and grandchildren would come and see me there and then leave me to continue my work without my needing to be too concerned about them and their on-going lives. It would be a time for me to really explore aspects of myself which I have never had the opportunity to do as I would have liked. It would be easy to say that these are nothing but pipe dreams, but the fact is that for many people today, dreams like this can be realized if they wish. Where our culture has fallen down is the emphasis which we lay on the immediate, on the possession of the latest gadget, on keeping up with the neighbours rather than the possibility of living on to an old age when such projects can be realized.

I should like to see a great expansion of the universities of the Third Age, and the introduction of other possibilities of work for the elderly. At the very least, there will be many tasks which can be carried out by older folk and which will give them interest and the feeling of still being able to make an input into their society. But I feel too that the increasing availability of information and knowledge which will be available to all as the information revolution sweeps on its irresistible way should not be denied to older folk, and that they should be encouraged to participate in the extraordinary opportunities offered by the computer age. It seems to me that one way of doing this might be to begin now to try and train those people who wish to work in the so-called 'helping professions' as counsellors, teachers and aides for the habilitation of the elders. I have remarked earlier in the book on the phenomenon of so many women wishing to become therapists and counsellors, and the fact that in our modern society, so much of the classical role of the wife and mother is being eroded. I would like to see the work of such organizations as Relate being extended into the field of working with the elderly, but not in terms so much of therapy as of facilitation.

It seems likely too, that as more and more people are enabled to leave the vast conurbations which we can now abandon in the wake of the changes in work habits and communications, then there emerges the need for the creation and recreation of smaller communities within which the men and women of the next millennium will live and work. I can foresee a very important role for the older person here, since they will become the guarantors and providers of many services in such small communities. Again, I think that some form of training which will provide older people with models for the work which will be available in the new dispersed small communities would be of great help. I am not thinking about anything terribly complicated here – having acquired a bookkeeping programme for my computer which cost little more than £100.00, I have recently been struggling to understand double entry accounts, something which I never had the time or energy to do before and therefore had to pay my accountants to do for me. It would be marvellous if I could find a retired accountant or bookkeeper who would help me work out the principles, so that I could be sure that I was working along the right lines. We would all benefit – he would have some work, I would save my accountant's fees, and my accountants would be freed up to do more interesting and challenging work such as thinking up new ways to outwit the Inland Revenue.

Naturally, it is a thankless task to try and predict the future. My friend Eric Trist who was one of the outstanding management consultants of his generation used to say that the reason that managers were given such huge salaries was that they had the task of planning for years ahead, but that anyone who pretended that they could plan for anything more than three to four years in any sphere of activity was talking nonsense. What we can do however, is to try and create a climate of opinion in which the sorts of development which I have been talking about in this book might happen. I would like to see a two-phase adult career available to people, with an option to retire from their primary careers very early, and the opportunity of relearning and redirecting themselves from the mid-forties on. There are times, certainly, when I am convinced that university is wasted on the young, and that mature students are far more rewarding to teach than are those in late adolescence, despite the power and speed of the intellectual uptake of the young people of today. It might help some of the pain and unhappiness which seems so endemic to so many in the course of the ageing process if, instead of feeling that they will soon be on the scrap heap and have very little to which to look forward, they can feel that not only will there be the opportunity to retrain themselves in ways which they now see they did not take for good conscious or unconscious reasons, but that what they produce will be acceptable and valued by society. In Robert Browning's *Rabbi Ben Ezra*, Browning, or rather the character in whose name he was speaking, refers to religion and the after-life, the contemplation of immortality and the cultivation of one's immortal soul when he says: 'Grow old along with me, The best is yet to be!'[24] I recognize that this is a very appropriate task for later life: what I have been trying to argue in this book is that it is possible to widen the range of possibilities for older people without losing either the spiritual or the economic gains of later life. I hope that a psychodynamically oriented approach to these problems will contribute to our understanding and reinforce what I feel is a necessary evolution in the understanding and elaboration of the phases of ageing as they happen to all of us.

Notes

1 Orville G. Brim, 'Theories of the male mid-life crisis', *Counselling Psychologist, 6* (1976), pp. 2–9.

2 Bernice Neugarten and G. Hagestad, 'Age and the Life Course' in *Handbook of Ageing and the Social Sciences*, ed., R. Binstock, and E. Shanas. New York: Van Nostrand, 1976.

3 Neugarten and Hagestad, 'Age and the Life Course'.

4 Carl G. Jung, 'The stages of life' in J. Campbell, ed., *The Portable Jung*. New York: Viking, 1933.

5 Figure reprinted from R. Nemiroff and C. Colarusso, *The Race Against Time: Psychotherapy and Psychoanalysis in the Second Half of Life*. New York: Plenum, 1985.

6 Nemiroff and Colarusso, *The Race Against Time*.

7 William Masters and V. Johnson, *Human Sexual Response*. London: Helmdale, 1966.

8 D. Guttman, 'Psychological Developments and Pathology in Later Life' in *New Dimensions in Adult Development*, ed., R. Nemiroff and C. Colarusso. New York: Basic Books, 1990.

9 Sheila A. Sharpe, 'The Oppositional Couple: A Developmental Object Relations Approach to Diagnosis and Treatment' in *New Dimensions in Adult Development*, ed., Nemiroff and Colarusso.

10 Joseph Kuypers and V. Bengston, 'Toward Competence in the Older Family' in *Family Relationships in Later Life*, ed., Timothy Brubaker. Beverly Hills: Sage, 1983.

11 S. Freud *On Psychotherapy*, in Standard Edition vol. VII. London: Hogarth, 1905.

12 *Life, Work and Livelihood in the Third Age: The Carnegie Inquiry*. Folkestone: Bailey, 1993.

13 Patrick Rabbit, 'Changes in Problem-Solving Ability in Old Age' in *The Psychology of Aging*, eds., James Birren and K. Schaie. New York: Van Rostrand, 1977.

14 B. Cohler and R. Galatzer-Levy, 'Self, Meaning and Morale Across the Second Half of Life' in *New Dimensions in Adult Development*, ed., Nemiroff and Colarusso.

15 Elliot Jacques, 'Death and the Mid-Life Crisis', *International Journal of Psychoanalysis, 46*, part 4, 1965.

16 George Pollock, 'Ageing or Aged: Development or Pathology' in *The Course of Life* eds., George Pollock and S. Greenspan. Bethesda: NIMH, 1980.

17 H. Peter Hildebrand, 'The Other Side of the Wall', *International Journal of Psychoanalysis, 15*, part 4, 1988.

18 Pearl H. M. King, 'Notes on the Psychoanalysis of Older Patients', *Journal of Analytical Psychology, 19*, (1974), pp. 22–37

19 Irvin D. Yalom, *Existential Psychotherapy*. New York: Basic Books, 1980.

20 H. Peter Hildebrand, 'A Patient Dying with Aids', *International Review of Psychoanalysis, 19*, part 4, 1992.

21 Yalom, *Existential Psychotherapy*.

22 Martin Grotjahn, 'The day I became old', *Lancet* (20 February 1982), pp. 441–2.

23 Ernest Jones, *Sigmund Freud: Life and Work, Vol III: The Last Phase*. London: Chatto, 1974.

24 Robert Browning, 'Rabbi ben Ezra' in *Dramatis Personae* in ed., I. Jack, *Poetical Works 1833–64*. London: Oxford University Press, 1970.

| Index